THE ENCYCLOPEDIA OF PSYCHOACTIVE DRUGS

IN 25 VOLUMES
Each title on a specific drug or drug-related problem

OVER-THE-COUNTER DRUGS

GENERAL EDITOR
Professor Solomon H. Snyder, M.D.
*Distinguished Service Professor of
Neuroscience, Pharmacology, and Psychiatry at
The Johns Hopkins University School of Medicine*

ASSOCIATE EDITOR
Professor Barry L. Jacobs, Ph.D.
Program in Neuroscience, Department of Psychology, Princeton University

---

SENIOR EDITORIAL CONSULTANT
Jerome H. Jaffe, M.D.
Director of The Addiction Research Center, National Institute on Drug Abuse

THE ENCYCLOPEDIA OF PSYCHOACTIVE DRUGS

OVER-THE-COUNTER DRUGS

Harmless or Hazardous?

PAUL SANBERG, Ph.D.

Ohio University

RICHARD M. T. KREMA

Ohio University

1986
CHELSEA HOUSE PUBLISHERS
NEW YORK
NEW HAVEN   PHILADELPHIA

SENIOR EDITOR: William P. Hansen
ASSOCIATE EDITORS: John Haney, Richard Mandell
CAPTIONS: Marian W. Taylor
EDITORIAL COORDINATOR: Karyn Gullen Browne
ART DIRECTOR: Susan Lusk
ART COORDINATOR: Carol McDougall
LAYOUT: Ghila Krajzman, Tenaz Mehta
PICTURE RESEARCH: Susan Quist, Ian Ensign

First Printing

Library of Congress Cataloging in Publication Data
Sanberg, Paul.
    Over-the-counter drugs.
    (The Encyclopedia of psychoactive drugs)
    Bibliography: p.
    Includes index.
    Summary: Examines psychoactive drugs which are
available without a doctor's prescription, discussing
which are effective and which are harmful.
    1. Drugs, Nonprescription—Juvenile literature.
2. Drugs—Effectiveness—Juvenile literature.
3. Drugs, Nonprescription—Toxicology—Juvenile literature. [1. Drugs,
Nonprescription]   I. Krema, Richard M.T.   . II. Title.   III. Series.
RM671.A1S36   1986   615'.1   85–17438

ISBN 0-87754-764-5

Chelsea House Publishers
Harold Steinberg, Chairman & Publisher
Susan Lusk, Vice President
A Division of Chelsea House Educational Communications, Inc.

Chelsea House Publishers
133 Christopher Street
New York, NY 10014

Photos courtesy of Bayer AG, The Bettmann Archive, Inc., Library of
Congress, National Library of Medicine, Julie Nichols, Susan Quist, UPI/Bettmann
Newsphotos.

CONTENTS

A careful consumer studies the label on a package of nonprescription medicine. Many drugstore shoppers mistakenly assume that all preparations available without a doctor's prescription are safe.

In the Mainstream of American Life

The rapid growth of drug use and abuse is one of the most dramatic changes in the fabric of American society in the last 20 years. The United States has the highest level of psychoactive drug use of any industrialized society. It is 10 to 30 times greater than it was 20 years ago.

According to a recent Gallup poll, young people consider drugs the leading problem that they face. One of the legacies of the social upheaval of the 1960s is that psychoactive drugs have become part of the mainstream of American life. Schools, homes, and communities cannot be "drug proofed." There is a demand for drugs—and the supply is plentiful. Social norms have changed and drugs are not only available—they are everywhere.

Almost all drug use begins in the preteen and teenage years. These years are few in the total life cycle, but critical in the maturation process. During these years adolescents face the difficult tasks of discovering their identity, clarifying their sexual roles, asserting their independence, learning to cope with authority, and searching for goals that will give their lives meaning. During this intense period of growth, conflict is inevitable and the temptation to use drugs is great. Drugs are readily available, adolescents are curious and vulnerable, there is peer pressure to experiment, and there is the temptation to escape from conflicts.

No matter what their age or socioeconomic status, no group is immune to the allure and effects of psychoactive drugs. The U.S. Surgeon General's report, "Healthy People," indicates that 30% of all deaths in the United States

Medicines made from herbs and other plant substances were widely used in the 18th and 19th centuries, but gradually synthesized drugs gained in popularity. Since the 1960s, however, herbal-remedy use has increased.

are premature because of alcohol and tobacco use. However, the most shocking development in this report is that mortality in the age group between 15 and 24 has increased since 1960 despite the fact that death rates for all other age groups have declined in the 20th century. Accidents, suicides, and homicides are the leading cause of death in young people 15 to 24 years of age. In many cases the deaths are directly related to drug use.

THE ENCYCLOPEDIA OF PSYCHOACTIVE DRUGS answers the questions that young people are likely to ask about drugs, as well as those they might not think to ask, but should. Topics include: what it means to be intoxicated; how drugs affect mood; why people take drugs; who takes them; when they take them; and how much they take. They will learn what happens to a drug when it enters the body. They will learn what it means to get "hooked" and how it happens. They will learn how drugs affect their driving, their schoolwork, and those around them—their peers, their family, their friends, and their employers. They will learn what the signs are that indicate that a friend or a family member may have a drug problem and to identify four stages leading from drug use to drug abuse. Myths about drugs are dispelled.

National surveys indicate that students are eager for information about drugs and that they respond to it. Students not only need information about drugs—they want information. How they get it often proves crucial. Providing young people with accurate knowledge about drugs is one of the most critical aspects.

THE ENCYCLOPEDIA OF PSYCHOACTIVE DRUGS synthesizes the wealth of new information in this field and demystifies this complex and important subject. Each volume in the series is written by an expert in the field. Handsomely illustrated, this multi-volume series is geared for teenage readers. Young people will read these books, share them, talk about them, and make more informed decisions because of them.

Miriam Cohen, Ph.D.
Contributing Editor

A French engraving portrays a 17th-century apothecary, or druggist, as a walking medicine cabinet. Societies all over the world have used and experimented with healing and mind-altering drugs since the beginning of recorded time. The Greeks, for example, had a form of aspirin 2,500 years ago, and marijuana was used medicinally as early as 3000 B.C.E.

INTRODUCTION

The Gift of Wizardry
Use and Abuse

JACK H. MENDELSON, M.D.
NANCY K. MELLO, PH.D.
Alcohol and Drug Abuse Research Center
Harvard Medical School—McLean Hospital

Dorothy to the Wizard:

"I think you are a very bad man," said Dorothy.
"Oh, no, my dear; I'm really a very good man; but I'm a very bad Wizard."
—from THE WIZARD OF OZ

Man is endowed with the gift of wizardry, a talent for discovery and invention. The discovery and invention of substances that change the way we feel and behave are among man's special accomplishments, and like so many other products of our wizardry, these substances have the capacity to harm as well as to help. The substance itself is neutral, an intricate molecular structure. Yet, "too much" can be sickening, even deadly. It is man who decides how each substance is used, and it is man's beliefs and perceptions that give this neutral substance the attributes to heal or destroy.

Consider alcohol—available to all and yet regarded with intense ambivalence from biblical times to the present day. The use of alcoholic beverages dates back to our earliest ancestors. Alcohol use and misuse became associated with the worship of gods and demons. One of the most powerful Greek gods was Dionysus, lord of the Underworld and god of wine. The Romans adopted Dionysus but changed his name to Bacchus. Festivals and holidays associated with Bacchus celebrated the harvest and the origins of life. Time has blurred the images of the Bacchanalian festival, but the theme of drunkenness as a major part of celebration has survived the pagan gods and remains a familiar part of modern society. The term "Bacchanalian festival" conveys a more appealing image than "drunken orgy" or "pot

13

party," but whatever the label, some of the celebrants will inevitably start up the "high" escalator to the next plateau. Once there, the de-escalation is difficult for many.

According to reliable estimates, one out of every ten Americans develops a serious alcohol-related problem sometime in his or her lifetime. In addition, automobile accidents caused by drunken drivers claim the lives of tens of thousands every year. Many of the victims are gifted young people, just starting out in adult life. Hospital emergency rooms abound with patients seeking help for alcohol-related injuries.

Who is to blame? Can we blame the many manufacturers who produce such an amazing variety of alcoholic beverages? Should we blame the educators who fail to explain the perils of intoxication, or so exaggerate the dangers of drinking that no one could possibly believe them? Are friends to blame—those peers who urge others to "drink more and faster," or the macho types who stress the importance of being able to "hold your liquor"? Casting blame, however, is hardly constructive, and pointing the finger is a fruitless way to deal with problems. Alcoholism and drug abuse have few culprits but many victims. Accountability begins with each of us, every time we choose to use or to misuse an intoxicating substance.

It is ironic that some of man's earliest medicines, derived from natural plant products, are used today to poison and to intoxicate. Relief from pain and suffering is one of society's many continuing goals. Over 3,000 years ago, the Therapeutic Papyrus of Thebes, one of our earliest written records, gave instructions for the use of opium in the treatment of pain. Opium, in the form of its major derivative, morphine, remains one of the most powerful drugs we have for pain relief. But opium, morphine, and similar compounds, such as heroin, have also been used by many to induce changes in mood and feeling. Another example of man's misuse of a natural substance is the coca leaf, which for centuries was used by the Indians of Peru to reduce fatigue and hunger. Its modern derivative, cocaine, has important medical use as a local anesthetic. Unfortunately, its increasing abuse in the 1980s has reached epidemic proportions.

The purpose of this series is to provide information about the nature and behavioral effects of alcohol and drugs, and the probable consequences of both their moderate use and abuse. The authors believe that up-to-date, objective information about alcohol and drugs will help readers make better decisions as to whether to use them or not. The information presented here (and in other books in this series) is based on many clinical and laboratory studies and observations by people from diverse walks of life.

Over the centuries, novelists, poets, and dramatists have provided us with many insights into the beneficial and problematic aspects of alcohol and drug use. Physicians, lawyers, biologists, psychologists, and social scientists have contributed to a better understanding of the causes and consequences of using these substances. The authors in this series have attempted to gather and condense all the latest information about drug use and abuse. They have also described the sometimes wide gaps in our knowledge and have suggested some new ways to answer many difficult questions.

One such question, for example, is how do alcohol and drug problems get started? And what is the best way to treat them when they do? Not too many years ago, alcoholics and drug abusers were regarded as evil, immoral, or both. It is now recognized that these persons suffer from very complicated diseases involving deep psychological and social problems. To understand how the disease begins and progresses, it is necessary to understand the nature of the substance, the behavior of the afflicted person, and the characteristics of the society or culture in which he lives.

The diagram below shows the interaction of these three factors. The arrows indicate that the substance not only affects the user personally, but the society as well. Society influences attitudes towards the substance, which in turn affect its availability. The substance's impact upon the society may support or discourage the use and abuse of that substance.

SUBSTANCE
(ALCOHOL OR DRUG)

PERSON ← → SOCIETY

Minnie Belle McAvoy, America's first licensed female pharmacist, mixes a prescription in her Manhattan drugstore in 1924. Before federal laws were tightened, "medicine" was often dispensed by unlicensed individuals.

Although many of the social environments we live in are very similar, some of the most subtle differences can strongly influence our thinking and behavior. Where we live, go to school and work, whom we discuss things with—all influence our opinions about drug use and misuse. Yet we also share certain commonly accepted beliefs that outweigh any differences in our attitudes. The authors in this series have tried to identify and discuss the central, most crucial issues concerning drug use and misuse.

Regrettably, man's wizardry in developing new substances in medical therapeutics has not always been paralleled by intelligent usage. Although we do know a great deal about the effects of alcohol and drugs, we have yet to learn how to impart that knowledge, especially to young adults.

Does it matter? What harm does it do to smoke a little pot or have a few beers? What is it like to be intoxicated? How long does it last? Will it make me feel really fine? Will it make me sick? What are the risks? These are but a few of the questions answered in this series, which, hopefully, will enable the reader to make wise decisions concerning the crucial issue of drugs.

Information sensibly acted upon can go a long way towards helping everyone develop his or her best self. As one keen and sensitive observer, Dr. Lewis Thomas, has said,

> "There is nothing at all absurd about the human condition. We matter. It seems to me a good guess, hazarded by a good many people who have thought about it, that we may be engaged in the formation of something like a mind for the life of this planet. If this is so, we are still at the most primitive stage, still fumbling with language and thinking, but infinitely capacitated for the future. Looked at this way, it is remarkable that we've come as far as we have in so short a period, really no time at all as geologists measure time. We are the newest, the youngest, and the brightest thing around."

A health fanatic pours himself a cup of "peptonized zebra milk." Some products in the multimillion-dollar nutrition market are no more effective than those satirized in this Puck *magazine cartoon.*

18

CHAPTER 1

THE DRUGGING OF AMERICA

Why should a person worry about taking a drug that can be purchased by anyone at the corner store and without a prescription? What does Anacin or Robitussin cough syrup, for example, have to do with drug abuse?

The general public has been led to assume that any drug made available without prescription has been thoroughly tested and is thus well established as safe and effective treatment for the ailment for which it is intended. In fact, the Food and Drug Administration (FDA) has not found evidence that this assumption is true for many over-the-counter (OTC) products. The FDA's OTC advisory panels, established about 10 years ago, have concluded that only approximately one-third of the ingredients in the 300,000 brands of OTC products studied were safe and effective for their intended uses.

Evaluating the safety and effectiveness of a drug requires rigorous scientific testing. Strict scientific assessments of the ingredients in OTC products, based on "double-blind" studies (discussed in Chapter 7), were initiated in the early 1970s. They are designed to ensure that the drug's effects are real rather than imagined and that they could not be produced by a placebo—a substance, such as sugar, that produces no noticeable effects.

In a double-blind study only the experimenter, but neither the administrator of the drug nor the patient, knows whether the ingested substance is a placebo or the actual drug. Therefore, the patient cannot know or be given any clues regarding the pill's actual content. If a statistically significant number of patients feel an effect no matter what is ingested, the experimenter can conclude that the "drug" is not effective. However, if the patient consistently notices an effect only when taking the drug, one can conclude that the drug is effective. Many of the approximately one-half million OTC products, composed of 500 to 1000 active ingredients, have not been studied in this fashion.

Many of the OTC products for which there is no proof of safety or efficacy do not present a serious health hazard for most people if taken in the recommended amounts and for the symptoms they are supposed to alleviate. But when these drugs are used in excess, or when they are used when they are not needed at all—and unfortunately this is the case for many people—they can become hazardous.

To understand fully a drug's hazards and potential for abuse, one must understand the drug itself. This book de-

Good News to the Sick.

Ver again∫t *Ludgate* Church, within *Black-Fryers* Gate-way, at *Lillies-Head*, Liveth your old Friend Dr. *Ca∫e*, who faithfully Cures the Grand P–, with all its Symptoms, very Cheap, Private, and without the lea∫t Hindrance of Bu∫ine∫s. *Note*, He hath been a Phy∫itian 33 Years, and gives Advice in any Di∫tem per *gratis*.

All ye that are of *Venus* Race,
Apply your ∫elves to Dr. *Ca∫e* :
Who, with a Box or two of PILLS,
Will ∫oon remove your painful ILLS.

A poster advertises the services of "Dr. Case," who was a notorious 18th-century quack. Prospective patients were assured that Dr. Case, "with a box or two of PILLS, will soon remove your painfull ILLS"—lines not very different from those used to advertise some of today's OTC drugs.

20

scribes the available OTC drugs, and their potential dangers and adverse effects.

When drug abuse is mentioned one often thinks of a person who takes recreational drugs—such as marijuana, cocaine, or heroin—to escape reality and get "high." However, drug abuse also includes the behavior of a person who takes more medication than is recommended or required to alleviate aches and pains. In fact, this type of drug taking can be just as dangerous as using heroin. For example, aspirin is often used to commit suicide. Taking too much of any drug, no matter what the initial motivation, nonetheless constitutes abuse.

In 1985 there is good reason to give this topic serious consideration. An ever-increasing number of people rely on one kind of OTC product or another just to get through the day. Several decades ago people showed a much higher degree of "frustration tolerance" than now and thus depended upon fewer drugs. Undoubtedly, part of the reason why they were able to put up with more aches and pains is that, in many cases, the drugs that could alleviate these symptoms were either not available or did not yet exist.

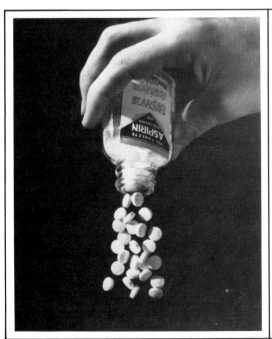

Aspirin is the most widely used drug in the United States. For most people it is a relatively safe, nonaddictive medication that effectively treats pain, fever, and inflammation. For others, especially those who misuse it, aspirin can cause ringing in the ears, nausea, heartburn, vomiting, internal bleeding, convulsions, and even death. More hospitalizations for adverse drug reactions are due to aspirin than to any other drug.

Thus they did not have the expectation of "instant relief" which many have today. In addition, the volume of advertising was much smaller, and consequently people had comparatively little information on what kinds of products were available.

But the situation has changed. Now, one expects there to be a drug solution for every discomfort, from a hangover to cancer, and over the years we have been convinced that it is available from OTC products. Television commercials are especially effective, as are magazine and newspaper ads and the anecdotal evidence of family and friends.

When it comes to taking drugs, children follow examples set by their parents. A very large proportion of parents take OTC and other drugs on a daily basis. Several studies have concluded that what influences whether or not children go on to abuse drugs is not so much the type of drug the parents take but just the fact that they take drugs. Parental use of any type of drug (pills, alcohol, or even coffee) tends to foster drug taking in the children. And perhaps because child rearing has generally been the duty of the woman, a child is much more likely to take drugs if the mother, rather than the father, uses drugs.

The belief that there is a drug for any ailment is often learned at home; drug-using parents may teach children their dangerous habits.

Table 1

Frequency of OTC Use	
FREQUENCY	% OF 2558 TEST SUBJECTS
Very often	8.0
Occasionally	37.3
Not very often	45.4
Never	9.3

SOURCE: Adapted from Johnson, R.E. and Rope, C.R., "Health Status and Social Factors in Non-prescribed Drug Use," *Medical Care*, 21:225–233, 1983.

In addition to relatives and friends, family doctors also regularly encourage the use of nonprescription drugs. A few years ago 600 American doctors participated in a study intended to evaluate the doctor's role in perpetuating OTC drug use. The results showed that physicians who were likely to prescribe prescription drugs also frequently recommended nonprescription (i.e., OTC) drugs.

People are overmedicated, not only in the United States but in most of the industrialized world. The average American household stocks 17 different OTC products which they use to treat 70% of their illnesses. The results of a questionnaire published in 1983 showed that in any 30-week period approximately 85% of all American families purchased at least one OTC drug. Table 1 shows the frequency with which people use OTC products. OTC drug manufacturers reported that between 1980 and 1981 there was a 12% increase in sales, and according to another report, published in September 1983, Americans annually spend somewhere between $4 billion and $8 billion on OTC products.

Case Study 1

Mike was an above-average 12-year-old who did well in school, enjoyed sports, especially swimming, and played chess exceptionally well for his age. Other than one unpleasant experience with marijuana, he was not into drugs at all.

One day, while playing pinball, a friend walked in, pulled Mike aside, and told him that he had gotten ahold of some "black beauties," a type of stimulant. He assured Mike they were safe because they were "real speed" made by a leading drug company. Besides, his friend insisted, they could turn you into a whiz at video games. Finally Mike was convinced, and they both ingested two pills.

It is four years later and Mike regularly buys "uppers" through the mail, usually 1000 at a time for $25. He sells them to friends and fellow students. Mike himself now takes a minimum of 4 "beans" or "leapers" each day, sometimes as many as a dozen. In addition he now smokes a few marijuana joints a week and drinks beer at parties. Often he amazes himself at how much he can drink when he is high on uppers. In fact, sometimes he gets so drunk that he does not remember what he is doing or where he is doing it. He cuts many classes at school and is failing several courses. Again and again his mother asks, "What is wrong with you?"

Case Study 2

Tammy, an exceptional 15-year-old high-school student, had been on the honor role twice. She had many friends and had been going steady with Rick for almost 2 months. But in spite of constant reassurance from friends and family, she did not believe that she was pretty. Tammy was convinced that she was disgustingly fat, though her father told her that 131 pounds for a 5′ 8″ girl was quite normal, especially since she was still growing. But she wanted to become a model, and models are supposed to be skinny. Just thinking about her "condition" made her depressed for long periods. All efforts at dieting failed. One day her attention was captured by a television commercial that promised a quick and easy method to get rid of excess weight. By using an OTC aid, she could lose 10 pounds or more in a few weeks—guaranteed!

In the pharmacy she gazed at the colorful boxes of diet-aid products, her dreams of a modeling career seemingly within reach. Tammy chose an extra-strength brand. She succeeded in losing 11 pounds in 16 days, but she regained the weight in the following week. She dieted again and managed to achieve her dream weight of 117 pounds, but this lasted for only 2 days. She tried other diet aids, by themselves and in various combinations, yet the pounds just would not stay off.

She began to have headaches and stomachaches, and often felt nauseous and irritable. The only time she had a good night's sleep was when she did not take her pills for a day or so. Then she began oversleeping and missing classes. The only way she was able to function at school or hold her weekend job was if she ingested up to 5 capsules at a time. Constantly irritable, Tammy finally lost her closest friends and gained the nickname "crabby Tammy."

Fashion model Leslie Hornby, better known as Twiggy, was the epitome of high style in the 1960s, when thin was "in." Trying to duplicate the then current look of emaciated chic, many women damaged their health with excessive use of weight-loss pills and starvation diets.

Only slightly less ancient than the common cold is the common-cold remedy. Here, an early 19th-century sufferer follows the medical advice of his day by soaking his feet and bundling up.

CHAPTER 2

COLD REMEDIES

An article recently published in an American medical journal told of a 23-year-old woman who decided to drink a full bottle, or 300 ml (milliliters), of Nyquil after she had run out of whiskey. Nyquil, an OTC cold remedy, contains 25% alcohol and includes 6000 mg (milligrams) of acetaminophen (a pain reliever), 7.5 mg of doxylamine succinate (an antihistamine), 6 mg of ephedrine sulfate (a decongestant), and 15 mg of dextromethorphan hydrobromide (a cough suppressant). The recommended dose for a cold is 30 ml, or about 2 tablespoons. Therefore, the woman consumed 10 times the recommended dose of this cold remedy. A few hours later after taking the Nyquil, the woman felt extremely nauseous and vomited repeatedly. Two days later she was admitted to a nearby hospital and diagnosed as having severe hepatitis and kidney failure.

Consuming cold remedies to achieve a positive psychoactive effect appears to be on the upswing. Alcohol-containing syrups and formulas (see Table 2) are the most commonly abused products—where else can a minor legally get a shot glass of 50 proof alcohol? People who drink these preparations to get intoxicated are running high risks of serious and often permanent damage to their liver and kidneys. In fact, the renal (kidney) failure in the 23-year-old woman was mainly due to the 6000 mg of acetaminophen, an ingredient that is relatively safe in recommended doses. Because she drank habitually she was more prone to the liver toxicity associated with high doses of this painkiller.

Consumers spend over $1 billion a year on the approximately 1000 different cold remedies available on the market. The four most popular cold remedies—Nyquil, Dristan, Robitussin, and Sinutab—alone account for yearly sales of over $150 million.

Clear Lungs and a Dry Nose

Many OTC cold remedies contain substances that manufacturers claim are *expectorants*. Expectorants loosen the mucus in the lungs that collects during a common cold or flu. Expectoration is a cough that brings up mucus (also called phlegm or sputum) and is beneficial because the coughed-up material contains particles of the infecting virus. According to an FDA advisory panel, evidence that available OTC ex-

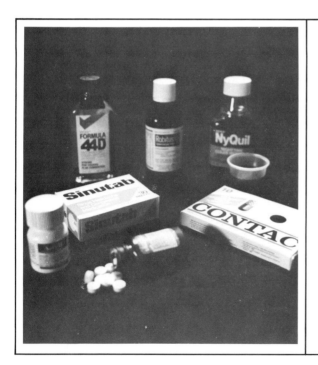

Doctors often say that a cold will last a week if medicine is given, and seven days if left alone. Although some of the popular cold medications—most of which contain alcohol—relieve cold symptoms, none will cure the cold.

Table 2

Alcohol-Containing Cough/Cold Remedies*						
NAME	% ALCOHOL	ACETAMIN-OPHEN	ANTIHISTAMINE	DECONGESTANT	COUGH SUPPRESSANT	EXPECTORANT
Cheracol	3				Codeine Phos.	Guaifenesin
Cheracol D	4.75				Dextromethorphan HBr	Guaifenesin
Congespirin	10	Yes		PPA		
Contac Jr.	10	Yes		PPA	Dextromethorphan HBr	
Coryban-D	7.5	Yes		Phenylephrine HCl	Dextromethorphan HBr	Guaifenesin
CoTylenol	7.5	Yes	Chlorpheniramine Maleate	Pseudoephedrine HCl	Dextromethorphan HBr	
Daycare	10	Yes		PPA	Dextromethorphan HBr	
Demazin	7.5		Chlorpheniramine Maleate	Phenylephrine HCl		
Dimetane	2.3		Brompheniramine Maleate	Phenylephrine HCl		
Dorcol	5			PPA	Dextromethorphan HBr	Guaifenesin
Dristan Ultra Colds	25	Yes	Chlorpheniramine Maleate	Pseudoephedrine HCl	Dextromethorphan HBr	
Formula 44	10		Doxylamine Succinate		Dextromethorphan HBr	
Formula 44D	10			PPA	Dextromethorphan HBr	Guaifenesin
Halls Cough Formula	22			PPA	Dextromethorphan HBr	
Novahistine Cold	5		Chlorpheniramine Maleate	PPA		
Novahistine Cough	7.5				Dextromethorphan HBr	Gauifenesin
Novahistine Cough & Cold	5		Chlorpheniramine Maleate	Pseudoephedrine HCl	Dextromethorphan HBr	
Nyquil	25	Yes	Doxylamine Succinate	Ephedrine Sulfate	Dextromethorphan HBr	
Pertussin	9.5				Dextromethorphan HBr	
Robitussin	3.5					Guaifenesin
Robitussin-CF	4.75			PPA	Dextromethorphan HBr	Guaifenesin
Robitussin-PE	1.4			Pseudoephedrine HCl		Guaifenesin
Sudafed	2.4			Pseudoephedrine HCl	Dextromethorphan HBr	Guaifenesin
Terpin Hydrate	39–44				Codeine	Terpin Hydrate
Vicks	5				Dextromethorphan HBr	Gauifenesin
Viromed	16.63	Yes		Pseudoephedrine HCl	Dextromethorphan HBr	

*Some of these products may no longer be available

29

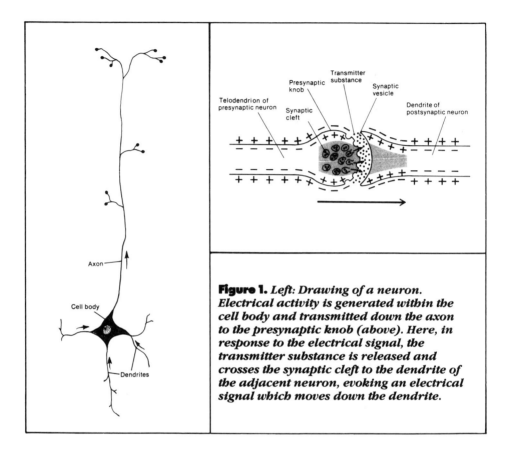

Figure 1. *Left: Drawing of a neuron. Electrical activity is generated within the cell body and transmitted down the axon to the presynaptic knob (above). Here, in response to the electrical signal, the transmitter substance is released and crosses the synaptic cleft to the dendrite of the adjacent neuron, evoking an electrical signal which moves down the dendrite.*

pectorants are genuinely effective is quite limited. The most widely used expectorant is guaifenesin (glyceryl guaiacolate), an active ingredient in Formula 44D. Other drugs that have been used as expectorants include ammonium chloride, terpin hydrate, iodides of calcium, camphor, menthol, ipecac syrup and fluid extract, turpentine oil, and chloroform. Most people are not aware that these drugs may not be effective, and that some, such as chloroform, ipecac fluid extract, and turpentine oil, are potentially dangerous.

The term *anticholinergic* is derived from the word acetylcholine (ACh). ACh is one of the chemical substances, or *neurotransmitters*, that acts as a messenger between neurons in the central nervous system. Neurons are specialized cells that have long wire-like protrusions called *axons* at one end. A bundle of axons constitutes a nerve. These axons communicate with other neuronal cell bodies, but their contact is not physical. There is a small space, called a *synaptic gap,* between the end of one axon and the cell body of the next neuron. When an electrical message reaches the end of the axon, the message has to cross this synapse, and this is accomplished by neurotransmitters such as ACh. The ACh molecule—a "translation" of the electrical charges— travels across the synaptic gap to specialized plug-ins called *receptor sites.* These are located on the numerous hair-like structures called *dendrites,* which protrude from the cell body of the next neuron. Once a sufficient quantity of ACh molecules becomes attached to these receptor sites, a new electrical charge is set up that travels along the axon of that neuron to the next neuron, and so on.

"Bitter Medicine," a painting by Flemish artist Adrian Brouwer (1606–1638). It was once widely believed that the worse a medicine tasted, the better it was for the patient. Today's pharmaceutical companies, however, work hard to make their products easy to take—and to sell.

Anticholinergic drugs alter the normal communication between neurons by binding to the receptor sites. Therefore, when ACh arrives it cannot deliver its message because the receptor sites are already full and transmitted ACh messages are never received. The result is that several bodily organs and structures—including parts of the brain, lungs, eyes, skeletal muscles, digestive system smooth muscles, and various other tissues—receive scrambled messages. Because of this binding property, anticholinergics can cause insomnia, agitation, disorientation, increased heart rate, blurred vision, constipation, hallucinations, and altered judgment.

Though a runny nose may be somewhat annoying, anticholinergic drugs should not be used to alleviate it. In fact, postnasal drip is beneficial. Just as coughing clears the lungs, mucus running from the nose helps to rid the body of foreign substances.

A member of the potato family, belladonna ("beautiful lady" in Italian), or the deadly nightshade, has been used since ancient times for cosmetic and medicinal purposes. Because the Romans considered enlarged eyes a sign of beauty, they used the drug, which causes pupil dilation, to enhance their appearance. When abused, belladonna can cause fatal reactions. Today atropine, which diminishes secretions and relieves spasms and pain, is extracted from belladonna and added to such medications as sleeping pills, anesthetics, anti-ulcer treatments, and OTC cold remedies.

The OTC anticholinergic drugs which have properties that dry up a runny nose are derived from the belladonna plant, also called deadly nightshade. Some of these drugs are atropine, scopolamine, and hyoscyamine. Belladonna alkaloids are found in older packages of cold remedies such as Contac Capsules. At recommended dose levels these drugs can have side effects. Drying up the air passages leaves the surfaces without protection, which can easily result in a dry, irritating, unproductive cough. Fatigue and/or excitation are common side effects due to the drug's neurological action. Dry mouth and thirst, constipation, a quickening of the heart, mental confusion, and blurred vision may occur in sensitive individuals.

In higher-than-recommended doses, anticholinergic drugs are quite toxic and can induce hallucinations, altered moods, and impairment of judgment. In addition, anticholinergics aggravate glaucoma, an eye disease characterized by an increase of pressure within the eye which ultimately leads to blindness. At doses considered safe for OTC drugs anticholinergics are not very effective in reducing excessive nasal discharge or watering eyes.

In the early 1980s the FDA prohibited the sale of any cold remedies that contain anticholinergics. Many consumers, however, still have cold medications that are months or even years old and contain anticholinergics. Though these drugs are no longer sold over the counter, there is no way to stop people from using these potentially dangerous substances once they have them in their possession.

To Clear the Airways

Bronchodilators, which act by dilating the bronchi of the lungs, clear the air passages and aid breathing. They are also intended to aid in expectoration and decongestion. The main category of OTC bronchodilator drugs are the ephedrine-related substances pseudoephedrine hydrochloride (HCl) and ephedrine sulfate, which have similar effects. Both drugs may cause hypertension (high blood pressure), restlessness, agitation, and, with high doses, psychotic behavior. Though bronchodilators are essential in the treatment of asthma, they are not recommended for the treatment of colds because of their potentially dangerous side effects.

Asthma Remedies

During an asthma attack a person has difficulty breathing. The remedies for asthma are drugs related to the adrenal gland hormone epinephrine, also known as adrenaline, and include ephedrine, isoproterenol (or isoprenaline), and metaproterenol. While the drugs are quite effective initially, *tolerance* develops, often rapidly. This means that to obtain relief from breathing difficulties, more and more of the drug is required. And with the increase in dosage comes side effects, such as nervousness and rapid heartbeat.

Metaproterenol became available as an OTC asthma remedy in the United States in March 1983. It was marketed under the name Alupent and heavily advertised on television as a "prescription-strength" product, which, in fact, it was. Soon after metaproterenol appeared as a nonprescription drug, it became apparent that the use of this product could be fatal. At recommended doses metaproterenol is an effective and essentially safe product. However, because of

Among the "mental alertness aids" offered in a magazine advertisement is ephedrine, which is often used to relieve symptoms of asthma. This OTC drug produces such side effects as trembling, insomnia, and rapid heartbeat.

the user's rapid development of tolerance, asthma sufferers are likely to abuse the drug.

Considering the extreme discomfort asthma patients may experience during an attack and the immediate relief offered by repeated inhalation of metaproterenol, that this drug is abused is not surprising. Unfortunately, when a person continuously inhales this drug the recommended doses are exceeded and progressive obstruction of the airways may be masked. This condition can lead to total respiratory collapse and even death. Because of its high abuse potential and the associated risks, metaproterenol is no longer available as an OTC drug.

Theophylline, formerly an antiasthmatic prescription drug, is now an OTC product. It is not, however, marketed as a single ingredient, but rather in combination with other substances. The doses of theophylline provided in the OTC product may not be sufficient to produce relief from an asthma attack, and therefore there is potential for abuse. The drugs with which theophylline is combined can be danger-

A hospital technician uses a spirometer to test the lung capacity of a five-year-old who has suffered from asthma since he was six months old. Bronchodilators metaproterenol and theophylline were both OTC drugs used to treat asthmatics. Though they can be dangerous and have a potential for abuse, only metaproterenol is no longer available as a nonprescription drug.

ous at the levels that are high enough to contain sufficient amounts of theophylline to have a therapeutic effect. For example, Bronkitin, Bronkotabs, and Primatene Tablets, in addition to containing theophylline, also contain various combinations of ephedrine, guaifenesin, and pyrilamine maleate or phenobarbital (a barbiturate—a category of drugs that depress the central nervous system and have dangerous side effects if taken in excess). Theophylline also has a narrow safety margin. Ingesting a quantity just slightly above the recommended dosage can be dangerous. Thus there is a very delicate balance between doses that are ineffectual and those that are hazardous. Drugs originally intended as safe medications can ultimately become a threat to one's health.

Antihistamines

Histamine is a chemical that is found in all body tissues, including the brain and the rest of the nervous system. In the central nervous system (CNS) histamine acts as a neurotransmitter, while outside the nervous system histamine plays an important part in inflammation and allergic reactions.

When a tissue is infected, damaged, or disturbed in any way, histamine is released from the cells in and around the affected area. Histamine's action on the surrounding capillaries allows larger amounts of fluid, protein, white blood cells, and *macrophages* (specialized cells that get rid of unwanted foreign substances and dead tissue) to pass from the capillaries and initiate the healing process. This sudden accumulation of substances is what is known as inflammation. Thus histamine and the associated inflammation play a very important role in the process by which the body prevents the spread of infection to neighboring tissues.

There are many people whose bodies are extremely sensitive to bug bites, pollen, and even dust. Their inflammatory defense mechanism is activated in response to any of these events. To most people a mosquito bite is only a minor irritation that results in a small welt. In allergic individuals (i.e., people with a highly sensitive system) the same bite may cause severe inflammation all over the body. If a nonallergic person enters a room where the pollen count has been artificially elevated to 10 times the highest concentration possible out in the open air, even he or she may sneeze, get congested, and have a runny nose and watery, itchy, red eyes. This is the body's way of getting rid of any pollen that has already invaded his or her body, and of preventing more of the pollen from entering his or her lungs and eyes. In allergic individuals much lower concentrations of pollen induce the same allergic reaction.

An antihistamine is a drug that inhibits the action of histamine and thus reduces or eliminates the allergic re-

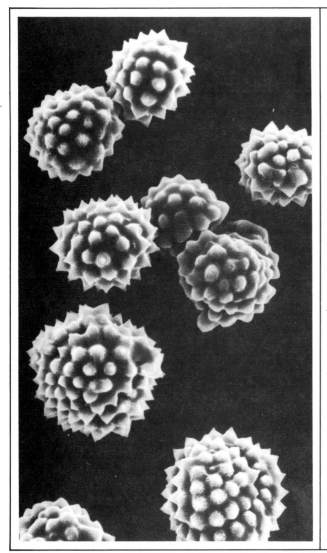

Pollen, released into the air by plants during their reproductive phase, appears to the naked eye as fine dust. However, when magnified 1,100 times, it becomes evident that pollen is actually composed of countless microspores. In those individuals who are highly sensitive, these jagged particles cause allergic reactions, characterized by sneezing, congestion, runny nose, and watery, itchy eyes.

sponse. Therefore, the annoying red eyes, sneezing, and runny nose are relieved. Most antihistamines are sedating and thus cause fatigue; they should be used cautiously if one is driving a car or operating any potentially dangerous machinery. OTC antihistamines that are widely used alone or in combination include diphenhydramine (Benadryl), doxylamine pyrilamine, chlorpheniramine (Chlortrimeton) and brompheniramine.

Nasal Decongestants

One of the most bothersome symptoms of a cold or flu is a congested, or stuffed, nose. To help get rid of this symptom the consumer can take a topical drug (inhalants, sprays, or drops) or an oral decongestant (pills or syrups). The disadvantages of pills and syrups is that they take much longer to act than inhalants, sprays, and drops, and they can also have many undesirable effects on the body. For example, if used topically (ingested through the nose) as recommended, ephedrine sulfate, phenylpropanolamine (PPA), and phenylephrine, three drugs used in nasal decongestants, produce the desired localized decongestant effect and do not affect the rest of the body.

All three of these drugs, however, affect the *catecho-*

In 1925 a news story announced the discovery of "a new way to cure colds"— a "gas-generating inhaler" inserted into a cup of tea.

lamines, neurotransmitters such as epinephrine (adrenaline) and dopamine. Therefore, if they are taken orally in high doses they can affect neurons and nerves throughout the whole body and cause hypertension, restlessness, agitation, sleeplessness, or even heart problems.

Topical nasal decongestants, if used for more than 2 or 3 days in a row, may cause *rebound congestion.* This has occurred when, after discontinuing drug use, the congestion actually becomes much worse than it was initially. The temptation is to resort again to the use of an inhalant to get rid of the congestion. This cycle can cause addiction to the inhalant, spray, or nose drops. The only solution is to stop using the inhalant altogether. When given the chance, the body can expel the irritant that is causing this symptom, and within a few weeks the congestion will disappear.

Cough Medicines

Antitussives are substances that act to inhibit an uncontrollable, dry, or unproductive cough. (The word "tussive" means related to, of the nature of, or pertaining to, a cough). A number of medications are available, and they include codeine, dextromethorphan, diphenhydramine hydrochloride (an antihistamine), various "combination" syrups, topical products (such as menthol-containing lozenges), and chest rubs, which are often composed of half a dozen different oils and extracts.

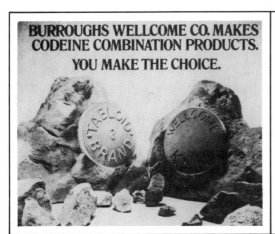

BURROUGHS WELLCOME CO. MAKES CODEINE COMBINATION PRODUCTS. YOU MAKE THE CHOICE.

Prescription drugs may not be advertised in consumer publications, but they frequently appear in medical journals. This ad offers doctors a choice between two codeine-containing cough suppressants. A note at the bottom warns that the pills "may be habit-forming."

The only truly effective cough suppressants are codeine and dextromethorphan. Codeine is one of the weakest narcotics (i.e., an opium derivative), which, apart from inhibiting the cough center in the brain, relieves pain and produces euphoria. Its inclusion in a number of cough remedies is, however, primarily due to its cough-suppressant effects. In fact, the amount of codeine contained in the recommended doses of cough remedies is not sufficient to produce pain-relieving effects.

A Cough is a Social Blunder

People who know have no hesitation in avoiding the cougher. They know that he is a public menace. They know that his cough is a proof of his lack of consideration of others.

And they know that he knows it too, so they are not afraid of hurting his feelings.

For there is no excuse for coughing. It is just as unnecessary as any other bad habit. For it can be prevented or relieved by the simplest of precautions—the use of S. B. Cough Drops.

S. B. Cough Drops are not a cure for colds. They are a preventive of coughing. True, they often keep a cough from developing into a sore throat or cold. And they are a protection to the public because they keep people who already have influenza, colds and other throat troubles from spreading them through unnecessary coughing. Have a box with you always.

Pure. No Drugs. Just enough charcoal to sweeten the stomach.

One placed in the mouth at bedtime will keep the breathing passages clear.

Drop that Cough
SMITH BROTHERS of Poughkeepsie
FAMOUS SINCE 1847

A cough drop manufacturer, which ran this ad in 1919, hoped to convince "coughers" that they could avoid serious "social blunders" by using its product, which also offered "protection to the public" by preventing "unnecessary coughing," for which there was "no excuse."

Codeine's potential for abuse, however, is comparatively high. Codeine-containing products may be abused in an attempt to reduce the coughing and pain due to colds, or in order to achieve the drug's euphoric effects. And excessively high doses and/or doses ingested too frequently can produce a condition of drug dependence. The liquid cold/cough formulas, which usually contain alcohol (see Table 2), are the forms of codeine most likely to be abused. Initially the person may be seeking the euphoric effects of either the codeine or the alcohol, but after repeated use of the combination he or she may become addicted to one or both of them. Since it is one of the weakest of the opium-

The poppy **Papaver somnivorum** *produces a milky juice, which is the source of the opiates: opium, morphine, codeine, and their derivatives. Even codeine, the weakest of these drugs, has a very high potential for abuse.*

derived analgesics, codeine has fewer and less severe side effects. Cough remedies that contain codeine include Ryna-CX Liquid, Cheracol, Cotussis, and Terpin Hydrate and Codeine Elixir. Though still sold over the counter in many parts of the country, because of their abuse potential, in some states codeine-containing medicines are available only by prescription.

Dextromethorphan, on the other hand, is a safe non-narcotic drug that suppresses coughing and is contained in most cough medicines. If too much is ingested, however, it will slow breathing. Unfortunately, dextromethorphan is usually only available in combinations that include up to four or five other ingredients. Because of this, when choosing a truly effective cough/cold medication, even the most cautious consumer is forced to ingest ineffective and potentially dangerous drugs to obtain the relief which a single, safe drug could provide.

Headache and Fever Medications

Analgesic is the technical word for pain reliever, and *antipyretics* are substances that reduce fever. Painkillers are discussed in greater detail in Chapter 3, but since many cough/cold remedies contain painkillers it is important to briefly consider them here.

The two main analgesics and antipyretics contained in OTC cold products are acetylsalicylic acid (aspirin) and acetaminophen. These two products are virtually the only analgesic/anti-inflammatory agents marketed as cold symptom relievers. Because a population has not yet been identified that is allergic to it, and because it does not irritate the stomach lining and cause bleeding (as aspirin may do), acetaminophen is presently by far the favored ingredient. However, unlike acetaminophen, aspirin reduces inflammation.

A high dose of acetaminophen can cause dangerous hepatotoxic (liver-damaging) effects. A common sequence of seemingly harmless events may lead to this condition. When a person consumes a product such as Nyquil he or she may not realize that it contains the analgesic acetaminophen, and so in addition he or she will take a few aspirins for pain, sometimes even chasing the aspirin with alcohol. Alcohol and aspirin are both stomach irritants, and the ingested combination can make the stomach lining painfully, even dangerously, irritated. This situation and others similar to it could be avoided if the drug user read *all* the ingredients in OTC drugs and considered the effects of each one before ingesting a combination that has the potential of being hazardous and even life-threatening.

Combination Cold Remedies

Of all the OTC medications available on the market, single-ingredient cold remedies constitute only a minor portion. Today the market is flooded with combination products that contain up to five different ingredients. Syrups, such as Nyquil, and the "extra-strength-guaranteed-to-relieve-10-symptoms" pills, such as Comtrex or Dristan Ultra Colds, contain many different drugs. This "shotgun" approach for treating a cold, which would probably clear up on its own within four days, is unwarranted and potentially dangerous.

An Arabian chemist distills medicinal wine for use as a cough suppressant. The illustration is from a book about botanical medicine by Pedanius Dioscorides, a 1st-century Greek physician whose work remained the authority on this subject for 1,500 years.

It may be informative to look at specific combinations in some detail. Both Comtrex and Dristan Ultra Colds contain acetaminophen, chlorpheniramine maleate, dextromethorphan hydrobromide (HBr), and either phenylpropanolamine (PPA) or pseudoephedrine HCl. And so, included in these drugs are an analgesic/antipyretic (acetaminophen) that reduces or eliminates fever, headache, and other pains; an antihistamine (chlorpheniramine maleate) that stops sneezing and watery eyes, but in addition causes drowsiness, low blood pressure, and headaches; an antitussive (dextromethorphan HBr) that inhibits coughing (though it may be "productive") and slows down breathing; and a decongestant (PPA or pseudoephedrine HCl) that may or may not clear breathing passages, but produces side effects such as elevated blood pressure and rapid breathing.

There are many reasons why this type of approach to treatment is unwarranted. Firstly, a person may not be suffering from all the symptoms—headache, sneezing, coughing,

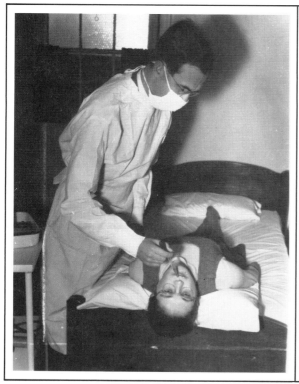

In the ongoing search for a common-cold cure, a virologist (a specialist in the study of viruses) at England's Harvard Common Cold Research Center puts drops containing a cold-causing virus in the nose of a volunteer subject. Researchers hoped to determine why only half of the people who were given the virus actually caught colds.

congested lungs, and a stuffed up nose—at the same time. Even if a person did have all these symptoms simultaneously, the possibility is remote that each drug contained in the medication exists in the correct dosage for the successful treatment of each of these symptoms. Because of this, he or she is likely to take additional doses just to get rid of the most bothersome symptom. Meanwhile, the person receives an overdose of the other ingredients. Flu symptoms are slightly different each time they occur. Sometimes the symptoms include a sinus headache and nasal congestion; sometimes a cough, a congested chest, and a mild fever; and other times just a runny nose and sneezing. Each symptom— and only if it is really unbearable—should and can be treated separately.

By using compound remedies to relieve one or two bothersome symptoms, people are taking excessive doses of too many drugs. If a person habitually does this each time he or she gets the flu, serious health problems may occur.

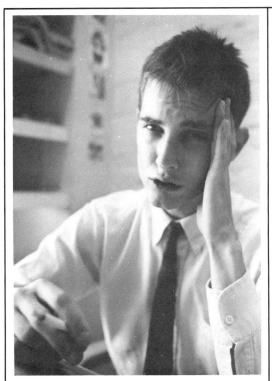

A bad case of the flu can make anyone miserable, but, in the long run, frequent use of the widely advertised, multipurpose OTC remedies to relieve flu symptoms is likely to be more harmful than helpful.

The 2 million aspirin tablets in this giant jar—a promotional exhibit at a Las Vegas exposition—represent less than one-third of the aspirin consumed by Americans every hour of every day.

CHAPTER 3

PAIN RELIEF

Pain is a signal that something is wrong. Without pain it would be difficult, if not impossible, to live. For example, without pain a person would not know when to remove his or her hand from a hot radiator and would thus suffer severe burns. There are many types of pain, such as headaches, muscle aches, and toothaches, all of which can be quite annoying. For many people these aches and pains are daily experiences.

Even though these pains are symptoms of some problem that needs correcting, it often seems simpler to eliminate the symptoms rather than combat the direct cause, which might in fact be serious. Because of the simplicity of this treatment and its ready availability, and because of the undeniable discomfort caused by the pain, more people purchase OTC painkillers than any other types of products. Sales for these drugs are over $1 billion each year. In 1981 the leading product was Anacin, with $112 million in retail sales, followed by Excedrin, with $56 million.

Among OTC painkillers, aspirin and acetaminophen, best known in the form of Tylenol, are the most popular. Other OTC pain relievers include salicylate, salicylamide, and salsalate, which are all closely related to aspirin. These will not be discussed at any length, since they are less potent representatives of the family of *salicylates* (see Fig. 2), and are, therefore, used much less frequently. Ibuprofen, sold under the brand name Advil and Nuprin, very recently joined the ranks of OTC products and may become very popular since it is quite potent. It has been a prescription product, known as Motrin of Rufen, for many years, so that much is now known about its safety and efficacy.

Phenacetin, a painkiller closely related to acetaminophen, was phased out as an OTC product between 1982 and 1983 because of its adverse effects, but because it may still exist in some households it will be discussed here.

The hands of an arthritis sufferer give evidence of the crippling effects of this disease, which torments millions. Aspirin provides some relief from the pain and swelling produced by arthritis.

Aspirin

In 1899, when Felix Hoffmann, a chemist at the Bayer Company, discovered a low-cost method of synthesis for acetylsalicylic acid, better known as aspirin, he started a veritable revolution in the OTC industry. Aspirin (acetylsalicylic acid, or ASA) is a member of a group of compounds called *salicylates* (see Fig. 2). Unlike the narcotic analgesics, which alter the perception of pain by acting on the central nervous system, aspirin acts locally at the source of the pain. The reduction of pain and inflammation is accomplished by vasodilation (dilation of blood vessels) and by a decrease in the production of *prostaglandins,* chemicals in the body that, along with histamines, are released during inflammation. When a fever is present, aspirin reduces body temperature by causing superficial (surface) blood vessels to dilate. But while this enables the body to dissipate more heat, it does not reduce actual heat production. In addition, research has shown that a fever is part of the body's mechanism to fight disease; therefore, reducing a fever actually slows down the healing process.

German Chemist Felix Hoffmann (1868-1946) paved the way for the commercial production of aspirin, which had first been synthesized in the mid-1800s. He became interested in the drug when he discovered that it gave his father relief from arthritis pain.

The major problem with aspirin is that it irritates the stomach lining, sometimes to the point of bleeding, and can lead to gastric and peptic ulcers. Prolonged use of aspirin may also interfere with the clotting of blood after an injury. To reduce aspirin's stomach-irritant properties, antacids have been included in a number of aspirin formulations. Bufferin, for example, contains two effective *buffers* which lower the stomach's acidity previously increased by aspirin ingestion. However, studies have repeatedly shown that with regards to stomach irritation, these products offer no significant advantage over plain aspirin taken with a glass of water.

People suffering from arthritis are highly prone to take near toxic doses of aspirin. Arthritis is characterized by inflamed joints which, when moved or put under stress, cause pain. Since aspirin reduces inflammation and pain, it is the drug most suggested for treatment of arthritis. Although the suggested adult dose is two 325-mg tablets four times a day, many sufferers will take much higher levels to reduce the inflammation and the pain. This amount of aspirin can cause salicylate toxicity, symptoms of which include dizziness, ringing in the ears, gastrointestinal problems, mental confusion, and bleeding. Clearly, these undesirable effects should be avoided as much as possible.

In 1975, 21-year-old Karen Anne Quinlan became the center of a highly publicized "right-to-die" case when her parents sought to discontinue life supports after she went into a coma. Tests showed that she had consumed a small amount of alcohol along with aspirin and, possibly, Valium. Even after the case was won and the life-support system was disconnected, she remained alive, unconscious until her death 10 years later.

Pepto-Bismol is widely advertised for the relief of an upset stomach. However, a recommended dose contains levels of salicylate equal to two aspirin. Therefore, if someone who is already taking high doses of aspirin—for the alleviation of rheumatoid arthritis, for instance—ingests Pepto-Bismol, he or she is unknowingly exposing him- or herself to a potential hazard. This combination of medications could result in a toxic salicylate level.

Believe it or not, some people take aspirin just to get high. Ten years ago there were stories that claimed that mixing aspirin with Coca-Cola was guaranteed to give you a "buzz." But by far the most common form of abuse is associated with taking far too much aspirin. This is usually done based on the incorrect assumption that if a small dose makes you feel better, then a larger one should make you

A 20th-century artist's interpretation of Days of the Papyrus Ebers, *a book first published in 1500* B.C.E., *shows an Egyptian doctor directing the preparation of medical potions. The book mentioned 700 drugs.*

feel great. This faulty reasoning has led to serious and even fatal overdoses. And yet, people obviously know that a high dose of aspirin can cause death. In 1985 aspirin, after barbiturates, is the drug of choice in suicide attempts.

Acetaminophen

Acetaminophen (N-acetylpara-aminophenol, or APAP) is as potent an analgesic and antipyretic as aspirin, but it has no effect on inflammation. As Fig. 2 illustrates, their chemical structures are also very similar. Acetaminophen has advantages over aspirin in that it does not necessarily irritate the gastrointestinal tract or other mucous membranes, and in recommended doses its side effects are negligible. Although acetaminophen is not anti-inflammatory, it is useful in alleviating arthritic pain.

A technician inspects blister-pack strips of aspirin-free tablets. The pills contain acetaminophen, an aspirin substitute that is increasingly used to combat arthritis pain.

Figure 2. *The chemical structure of four painkillers. All have a central benzene ring to which are attached additional atoms, which determine each one's particular characteristics. Note the similarities between aspirin and salicylate and between acetophenetidin and acetaminophen.*

SOURCE: Adapted from *Review of Medical Pharmacology.* F. H. Myers, E. Jawetz and A. Goldfien (Eds.), Los Altos: Lange, 1978.

Aspirin and Acetaminophen Compared

The pharmaceutical industry has been spending millions of dollars in advertising campaigns in the aspirin-versus-acetaminophen controversy. Many people who are allergic to aspirin or are predisposed to its stomach-irritating properties have been made aware of the acetaminophen alternative. However, many of the pharmaceutical companies have marketed both aspirin and acetaminophen and given them similar names. For example, Anacin contains aspirin, while Anacin-3 contains acetaminophen; and Congespirin Chewable Cold Tablets contain aspirin, while Congespirin Cold Medicine contains acetaminophen. This practice has made the process of acquiring accurate information and making intelligent decisions that much more complicated.

The major disadvantage of acetaminophen use is its potential for overdose toxicity. Though at recommended doses and frequency it poses no dangers, high doses can cause severe and sometimes fatal liver damage. On the other hand, even extremely high doses of aspirin, which can cause hallucinations, convulsions, and coma, are not likely to be fatal if treated in time. Long-term use of acetaminophen at recommended doses has not as yet been shown to be hazardous—hepatotoxicity usually only develops from massive overdoses. Long-term aspirin use, however, can result in gastrointestinal disorders. On the other hand, aspirin has the advantage over acetaminophen of being able to reduce inflammation as well as pain; acetaminophen only relieves the pain.

Recent evidence suggests that aspirin may have beneficial effects in addition to its pain-relieving and anti-inflammatory effects. Regular use of aspirin seems to prevent the development of senile cataracts and the deterioration of the eye lens. It is also thought to be effective in the treatment of myocardial infarction (i.e., heart muscle degeneration due to inadequate blood flow), and in reducing the incidence of reinfarction. It has also been used successfully in alleviating transient ischemic attacks (i.e., decreased blood supply to localized tissues). In infarction and ischemia treatment, for some as yet unknown reason, men seem to benefit more than women.

Acetaminophen has only been on the market for 30 years (whereas the family of salicylates was first identified in 1829, and its most prominent member, aspirin, was isolated 70 years later). Because of its recent emergence, not all of acetaminophen's positive and negative effects have been determined.

In 1982 Tylenol, the most popular OTC form of acetaminophen, was temporarily withdrawn from the market after several of its users had mysteriously died. They were discovered to have been poisoned by cyanide, which had been inserted into Tylenol packages after they had been placed on store shelves. Later that same year the drug was reintroduced in triple-sealed packages.

Every year in the United States thousands of children accidentally overdose on aspirin or acetaminophen, sometimes with fatal results. Analgesics manufactured for children are usually sugar-coated, or even "chewable," like candy. Many youngsters, unaware that the pills are medicine, do in fact eat them as if they were candy.

The aspirin/acetaminophen controversy has had the beneficial effect of bringing the possible health hazards of aspirin use to everyone's attention. Since the most common problem is stomach irritation, the drug manufacturers have provided the consumer with a wide choice of coated pills and capsules. Unfortunately, though coated pills may offer some protection for the mucosal lining of the mouth and

Because children are naturally both curious about and imitative of their parents, an unlocked medicine cabinet containing drugs—either prescription or OTC—is an open invitation to tragedy.

esophageal tube, they do not protect the stomach. Despite warnings, many people still take regular, uncoated aspirin tablets without any liquid. This practice has an effect on the mouth and esophageal lining similar to drinking slightly diluted hydrochloric acid. Aspirin is called acetylsalicylic *acid* because it *is* an acid, and a pretty strong one at that. Therefore, whether coated or not, aspirin should always be ingested with water or milk which dilutes it, but not with alcohol, which by itself can damage the stomach lining.

Since aspirin- and acetaminophen-containing products are the medications that are by far the most widely advertised and "prescribed" by both the media and physicians, and because these products can successfully treat the majority of aches and pains, they are often taken indiscriminately. To ensure that they are equipped to deal with minor ailments at all times, most American households stock aspirin- and/or acetaminophen-containing remedies. In theory there is nothing wrong with having these medicines on hand. One just has to exercise self-control and use them wisely. Firstly, their accessibility poses a danger for minors, who may unknowingly and indiscriminately take them as candy. Secondly, even responsible adults, when they are not feeling up to par, are likely to take anything readily available and not necessarily what is therapeutic.

The size of a recommended dose is determined from careful scientific studies. "One spoonful" means just that; two may be dangerous.

This practice can lead to psychological as well as to physical dependence. A high percentage of liquid OTC cough and cold remedies contain up to 600 mg of acetaminophen per spoonful, the common recommended dose. But quite frequently the recommended spoonful turns out to be a couple of "slurps" out of the bottle, a few times a day. More or less naively, many individuals do this and thus invite serious health problems.

Phenacetin

APC, A.S.A. Compound, and Os-Cal-Gesic are three pain relievers that contain phenacetin. However, it is not likely that they can be found in a store. Phenacetin is very closely related to acetaminophen, but despite this close chemical relationship phenacetin has been proven to be very dangerous. It has been identified as a carcinogen, and its prolonged use has been strongly correlated with a high incidence of kidney disease and anemia. In addition to its analgesic effect it can also cause drowsiness and mild euphoria.

Because of its sedative and euphoric effects and its reputation as an anxiety reliever, phenacetin has a high abuse potential. This and other dangers were clearly recognized in the mid-1970s, but it was not until August 1982 that the decision was made to remove it from the market within one year. Phenacetin is mentioned here because it is possible that many households still have products which contain it. Because of their dangerous side effects, products containing phenacetin should be thrown away.

Ibuprofen

Ibuprofen, a new OTC pain reliever, is currently receiving great media coverage. To accent its beneficial qualities, the advertisements report that at higher doses the active ingredient ibuprofen is classified as a prescription drug. Products such as Advil or Nuprin contain this ingredient. In recommended dosages ibuprofen is as effective an analgesic as aspirin or acetaminophen, but not superior; its anti-inflammatory effects, though, are inferior to aspirin's. In higher doses, however, ibuprofen is a more powerful pain reliever. Compared to aspirin, ibuprofen does seem to cause a lower incidence of gastrointestinal irritation and bleeding. Because it is new to the OTC market, there is yet no evidence of its abuse. Nevertheless, it is likely that it could be abused in ways similar to that described for aspirin.

Codeine

When found in OTC products, codeine is marked almost exclusively as a cough suppressant, and always in a low-ratio combination with other ingredients (see Chapter 2). Nonetheless, it is also a potent analgesic. When an antitussive product such as Cheracol, which contains 10 mg of codeine, is used in recommended doses, and only for its intended purpose, the analgesic properties are not very strong. When prescribed as an analgesic, however, the minimal effective dose range is 30 mg–65 mg. Codeine-containing OTC products may cause sedation and can, when used to excess,

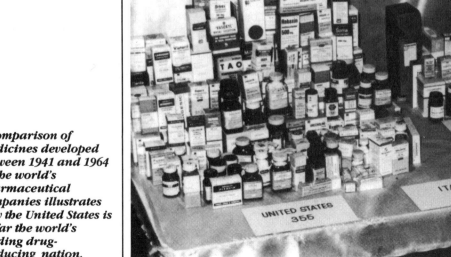

A comparison of medicines developed between 1941 and 1964 by the world's pharmaceutical companies illustrates how the United States is by far the world's leading drug-producing nation.

produce analgesic effects. The previously mentioned problem of overdosing on the other ingredients of a combination product is also of major concern here. But the greatest hazard that results from using codeine for its pain-relieving effects is the relatively high addiction potential.

Pain Reliever Boosters

Caffeine and many of the antihistamines are often added to painkillers to enhance their effects. When used for this purpose these other drugs are called adjuvants. Since practically no evidence exists for the effectiveness of antihistamines in this role, they will not be included in this discussion. The evidence that caffeine enhances the pain-relieving effect of analgesics (e.g., aspirin and acetaminophen), though not conclusive, is much stronger than it is for antihistamines.

Caffeine (trimethylxanthine) is found in coffee, tea, Coke,

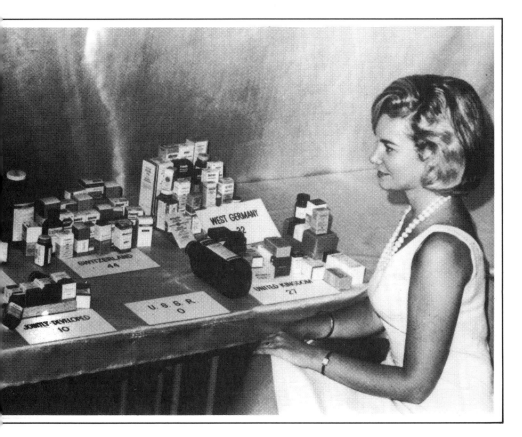

Pepsi, and chocolate-containing foods. It has mild CNS-stimulating properties, and is often sold over the counter in pill form alone (i.e., No Doz) or in combination with PPA or ephedrine, and advertised as either a stimulant or diet aid. Caffeine appears to exert its CNS-stimulating effects by blocking *adenosine* receptors. Adenosine is another chemical thought to be a neurotransmitter.

As an ingredient in painkillers caffeine is supposed to enhance the overall analgesic effect. However, some experts claim that it is useless and, in fact, a hazard. An editorial in the *Journal of the American Medical Association* maintained that most previous studies investigating caffeine's

Participating in an American ritual, a Rhode Island café proprietor pours coffee for a customer. The United States consumes more coffee than any country in the world. In 1984 the annual consumption of this caffeine-laden beverage reached 10.2 pounds per person in the nation.

enhancement of aspirin or acetaminophen used too low a dose of caffeine, i.e., 32 mg–64 mg. One study found that 1.4 times as much aspirin or acetaminophen is required to equal the analgesic effect of a combination of a given amount of either drug and 65 mg of caffeine. Because the 65 mg of caffeine was contained in each tablet of painkiller, a normal dose of 2 or 3 tablets would contain 130 mg or 195 mg of caffeine, equivalent to 1½ to 2½ cups of coffee (see Table 4,). Although it is true that 200 mg of caffeine can usually be tolerated by most people, problems can arise.

People often take up to a dozen painkillers in a day to subdue severe cold symptoms, headaches, or toothaches. This means that they may be ingesting up to 780 mg of caffeine. Combined with other sources of caffeine, their total daily caffeine intake may be more than 1000 mg. To get this much caffeine one would have to drink 7 cups of strongly brewed coffee.

Caffeine, like so many other drugs, can cause physical dependence. For example, someone who habitually drinks 3 to 6 cups of coffee each day during the work week, but only 1 or 2 cups on weekends may experience "migraines," an uncomfortable withdrawal symptom. The brain's adenosine receptors, accustomed to their daily "caffeine fix," respond to the decrease of caffeine and a headache results. Most people are not aware that just drinking their usual amount of coffee would alleviate the discomfort, and instead they take painkillers. In fact, they will probably discover that such caffeine-containing painkillers as Excedrin or Anacin provide the most relief for them.

Maintaining such high levels of caffeine is not healthy (see Chapter 4), and alleviating weekend caffeine-withdrawal headaches with caffeine-containing remedies perpetuates the coffee/caffeine addiction. The smart and economical way out of this vicious cycle is to cut down on coffee consumption.

Combination Products

Products with two or more active ingredients seem to appeal to the general public. This is as true for cold remedies as it is for painkillers. At first glance, combining aspirin, acetaminophen, and caffeine in order to enhance the overall analgesic effect does not seem unreasonable. And there are an appreciable number of products on the market that contain two or more analgesics in addition to other active ingredients (e.g., BC, Cystex, Excedrin Extra Strength, and Vanquish).

When only pain is the issue, a "shotgun" approach makes some sense. Headaches, toothaches, backaches, and cramps obviously have different causes, but the symptom is the same—pain. However, the subjective experience of the pain might be different. Headaches alone can vary in intensity, specific location, duration, and quality (i.e., dull, throbbing, sharp, or piercing). Because of the wide range of sensations and because no product claims to relieve a specific type of pain, people often conclude that a product containing two or three different painkillers is much more likely to alleviate the type of pain from which they are suffering.

Though there have been numerous studies, none has concluded that combination products are significantly more effective in reducing pain than either acetaminophen or aspirin alone. Therefore, there is no reason to risk the combined side effects of these products.

Anxious to relieve symptoms as quickly as possible, many drug users ingest combination products and risk the combined side effects. There is no solid evidence that such combinations increase effectiveness.

Menstrual Pain

Prior to a woman's menstrual period it is not uncommon for her to suffer from what is called *premenstrual syndrome.* This condition is characterized by fluid retention, or bloating, sensitive or painful breasts, and irritability. And during actual menstrual bleeding uterine contractions may cause severe cramps and pain. To eliminate these symptoms many women turn to various products specifically marketed to treat premenstrual syndrome. Examples include Pamprin, Midol, and Aqua-Ban. Most of these products contain aspirin or acetaminophen to relieve pain, and a diuretic to reduce fluid retention. However, none of the ingredients, other than the painkillers, have been proven effective in treating premenstrual syndrome.

In fact, the best way to reduce fluid buildup is to decrease salt intake for a week or so before menstruation. If this does not help, professional medical care should be sought. Ibuprofen has proven to be more effective in relieving menstrual cramps than aspirin or acetaminophen, though there have been reports of fluid retention associated with high doses.

Female apothecaries prepare herbal medicine in ancient Egypt. In treating "women's complaints" over the centuries, druggists have used potions containing many varieties of herbs, belladonna, and other potent substances. The major ingredient of "Lydia Pinkham's Organic Compound," a popular American medicine for women in the early 1900s, was cocaine.

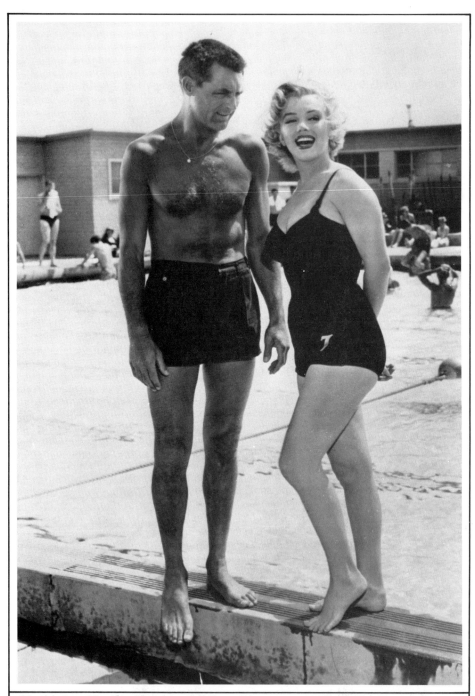

Movie stars Marilyn Monroe and Cary Grant pose in the 1950s. Monroe's voluptuousness, then much admired, would today be considered unstylish. In the 1980s women struggle to be thin, sometimes with the aid of drugs.

CHAPTER 4

STIMULANTS AND DIET AIDS

The terms "overweight" and "obese" mean different things to different people. However, it is generally accepted that being overweight or obese refers to the condition of exceeding acceptable weight standards for a given height. Although sometimes total body/water calculations or skinfold thickness are used, the most common way to determine if one's weight falls within an acceptable range is to compare it with the figures on an ideal weight table (see Table 3). Regardless of the criteria used, it is safe to say that in 1985 20% of all Americans weigh more than they should.

In the 1950s it was common for doctors to prescribe amphetamines (also known as "speed" or "uppers") for obesity. And frequently they were given to depressed patients, who lacked the motivation to function normally. When amphetamines were prescribed as anorectics (appetite suppressants), initially they did help the patient lose weight, but tolerance rapidly developed, necessitating higher doses of amphetamine to produce the desired effect. When increasing daily dosages were prescribed, the dieter was able to maintain the new weight, but not without paying the price.

The situation is like running high-octane racing fuel in a 1969 Volkswagen. At first the car will drive as if it were

Table 3

Ideal Weight Table				
HEIGHT (ft, in)	MEN'S WEIGHT (lb)		WOMEN'S WEIGHT (lb)	
	AVERAGE	ACCEPTABLE WEIGHT RANGE	AVERAGE	ACCEPTABLE WEIGHT RANGE
4 10			102	92–119
4 11			104	94–122
5 0			107	96–125
5 1			110	99–128
5 2	123	112–141	113	102–131
5 3	127	115–144	116	105–134
5 4	130	118–148	120	108–138
5 5	133	121–152	123	111–142
5 6	136	124–156	128	114–146
5 7	140	128–161	132	118–150
5 8	145	132–166	136	122–154
5 9	149	136–170	140	126–158
5 10	153	140–174	144	130–163
5 11	158	144–179	148	134–168
6 0	162	148–184	152	138–173
6 1	166	152–189		
6 2	171	156–194		
6 3	176	160–199		
6 4	181	164–204		

new, but soon troubles such as overheating of the upper cylinders (a condition aggravated by continued use of the high-octane fuel) will develop. Similarly, a person ingesting increasing doses of amphetamine will begin exhibiting psychotic-like symptoms (often indistinguishable from paranoid schizophrenia): heart palpitations, nervousness, agitation that can lead to violence, digestive problems, and, as the amphetamine wears off, depression. The "speed freaks" of the late 1960s and early 1970s were living testimony to the side effects of prolonged amphetamine use.

The chances are just as high that these same side effects will occur when amphetamine is prescribed to alleviate depression or given to a person to increase the motivation to cope with his or her daily problems. Simply, the human body functions better for a little while, but then, every system begins to exhibit symptoms of being overworked.

Whether amphetamines are used to combat lethargy or obesity, only short-term relief is accomplished. As past studies have shown, even patients who have every intention of using the amphetamine as prescribed find themselves taking greater and greater amounts and seeing a dozen or more doctors to obtain prescriptions for amphetamines. And to pay for the many office visits, many users entered the black market and sold a portion of their pills for more than they themselves had paid. The profit easily covered their own costs.

Physicians and the public finally became aware of the amphetamine-related problems. As a result, tighter restrictions were enforced. In the 1970s there was a steady decline in the number of prescriptions for amphetamines. In 1971 the pharmaceutical companies sold close to $12 billion worth of amphetamines compared to sales of $2 million in 1981.

Substitutes for Amphetamines

It is important to understand the effects of amphetamine, a prescription drug, for two reasons. Firstly, today people are buying OTC diet aids and stimulants for exactly the same reasons they had previously bought amphetamines: to use them to lose weight, to feel energetic and stay awake, and to

Photo by John Giorno

William Burroughs, Jr., (right) posing with his father, the writer William S. Burroughs, was greatly influenced by the Beat Generation's insatiable thirst for extreme experiences. At 33 years old he died after a life of drug (especially amphetamine) abuse.

Table 4

Caffeine Content in Common Beverages		
AMOUNT	BEVERAGE	CAFFEINE CONTENT (mg)
1 cup	Percolated coffee*	80–150
1 cup	Instant coffee	50–75
1 cup	Decaffeinated coffee	3–6
1 cup	Tea*	20–100
12 oz	Cola	50

*Caffeine content depends on brewing method.

get "high," and to sell them on the black market for a profit. Secondly, the ingredients of these OTC drugs can produce similar types of dangerous side effects.

How did this situation come about? Today doctors are very hesitant to prescribe amphetamines for any reason. Studies have shown that for the average person, the only way to keep excess pounds off is to use common sense. For most of us who lead relatively sedentary lives it would be wise to exercise more and eat less. For those who cringe at the thought of any kind of prolonged, sweaty activity, taking a pill is more tempting.

One television advertisement claims that their product will allow you to "lose pounds while you sleep." They even offer a money-back guarantee. So why not at least try it? Though this claim may be enticing, there is no evidence to support it.

Many people would also prefer to take an "energy" pill to deal more effectively with their day-to-day problems rather than to invest greater effort in developing more productive sleeping, working, and recreational habits. Pharmaceutical companies are quite aware of our weaknesses and use their knowledge to create seductive advertisements that promise easy solutions. They offer a wide variety of products, but most of them contain the same basic ingredients: caffeine, phenylpropanolamine (PPA), and ephedrine derivatives (ephedrine sulfate, ephedrine hydrochloride, and pseudo-ephedrine.)And in many ways these drugs are similar to amphetamines.

Caffeine

Caffeine is a stimulant used by people around the world. It is a major ingredient in coffee, which is why people drink it to get going in the morning and to keep them going when they get tired. The caffeine content of some common beverages is listed in Table 4. Derived from a class of drugs called *xanthines,* caffeine is a central nervous system stimulant that specifically stimulates the brain. It has been associated with anxiety, heart disease, gastrointestinal irritation, and ulcers.

Stimulants and diet pills contain up to 325 mg of caffeine per tablet or capsule. This means that even if one were to abstain from all other sources of caffeine (which is often difficult, since many drinks, foods, and other OTC and prescription drugs also contain caffeine), the two diet pills a day would provide an amount of caffeine equivalent to about five cups of coffee. Because the potential for ingesting a large amount of caffeine is very great, the risk of suffering from the hazardous side effects increases.

These three scenes from popular comics illustrate some of the effects of amphetamine abuse: paranoia (top, left); slurred speech and talkativeness (left); and psychosis, including hallucinations and violent behavior.

Caffeine-containing products often lack correct and/or adequate information regarding their effects. No Doz, for example, contains only one ingredient—100 mg of caffeine per pill. However, the manufacturer claims that No Doz is non-habit-forming. In fact, this may not be true. Caffeine use leads to dependence—a condition in which the body has adapted to certain daily levels of caffeine and, in fact, has come to depend on them. When caffeine levels abruptly drop, the body reacts, producing withdrawal symptoms characterized by uncomfortable headaches. Therefore, any products containing caffeine—including painkillers and cold remedies—have the potential to be habit-forming.

Ephedrine

Ephedrine, widely used in Chinese folk medicine, was introduced to the West in 1924. It is a *sympathomimetic* drug, which means that it mimics sympathetic nerve stimulation.

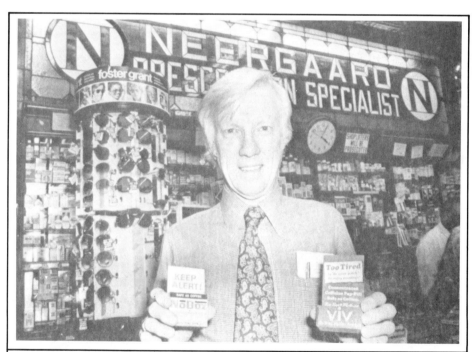

An all-night drugstore owner displays packages of caffeine-containing No Doz and Viv, which reportedly sell well between midnight and 5 A.M. High doses of caffeine can be extremely toxic.

The sympathetic nervous system elicits responses of alertness, excitement, and alarm, and controls the expenditure of energy necessary during an emergency. Sympathetic activation increases heart rate and raises the blood flow to the muscles. The blood vessels supplying the skin and stomach muscles constrict since these parts of the body are not needed to deal with an emergency. And finally, sympathetic activation stimulates the brain so that a person can think and react more quickly. Compared to caffeine, ephedrine's stimulant properties are much more pronounced.

Ephedrine is still used primarily to alleviate the symptoms of asthma (see Chapter 2). Asthma sufferers who ingest ephedrine 3 to 4 times a day commonly experience anxiety, agitation, tremulousness, and insomnia. This drug has also been linked to heart disease and cerebral hemorrhage (bleeding). In very high doses ephedrine, like amphetamine, is capable of producing psychoses.

A pharmacy in San Francisco's Chinatown. Like many other drugs used today, ephedrine, a sympathetic-nerve stimulator, was originally discovered centuries ago by the Chinese and widely used in folk medicine.

PPA

Almost all diet aids on the market contain phenylpropanol-amine, or PPA, whereas very few contain ephedrine. Amphetamine, ephedrine, and PPA (illustrated in Figure 3) all belong to the drug class *phenylisopropylamine.* PPA has many of the positive and negative effects of ephedrine. In the past few years, however, increasing numbers of people have begun to use diet aids to get high. To achieve this they may "pop" up to a dozen pills at a time. There is some evidence that high doses of PPA can cause the destruction of skeletal muscle. Taking high doses does seem to be a dangerous way to lose weight.

The Consumer and the Market

Diet aids, when compared to essentials such as soap or toothpaste, are easier to spot in the store—they are even displayed like candy at check-out counters. Manufacturers create catchy names—such as Control, Dexatrim (the 1984

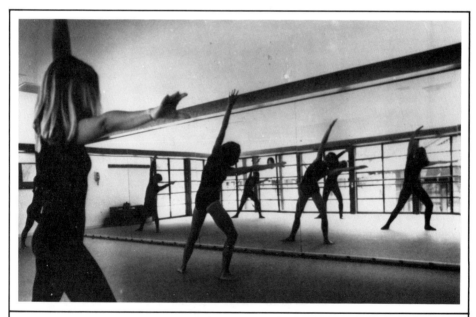

Despite the claims of drug companies, only regular exercise and a proper diet have proven to be safe and reliable ways to contain weight.

AMPHETAMINE

PHENYLPROPANOLAMINE

EPHEDRINE

Figure 3. *The chemical structures of phenylpropanolamine, or PPA, amphetamine, and ephedrine. All three, very similar in chemical composition, belong to the drug class phenylisopropylamine and produce extremely dangerous side effects.*

SOURCE: Adapted from Mueller, S. M., "Phenylpropanolamine, A Nonprescription Drug with Potentially Fatal Side Effects." *N. Eng. J. Med.* 308:653, 1983.

best-seller), Dietac, Maxi-Slim, Permathene, and Thinz-Span—in an attempt to lure the consumer. And television ads are cleverly designed so that any viewers thinking themselves overweight feel almost guilty for not at least giving the diet aids a try. It should not be at all surprising to learn that in 1982 Americans spent $220 million on diet pills.

Some of these OTC "miracle workers" are often hailed as containing certain drugs in the "maximum strength available without a prescription." Unfortunately, this statement is often quite true. Not only are caffeine, ephedrine, and PPA potent drugs, but on numerous occasions they have also proven to be dangerous. Even at recommended doses the drugs have potentially harmful side effects.

One has to remember that these drugs are being marketed to fill the gap created when amphetamines became difficult to obtain. This is why the pharmaceutical companies that manufacture these products take great care to make them look like prescription amphetamine pills. When they first came on the market, these *look-alikes* (see also Chapter 6) were sold to the naive drug user as "speed." Today, though most users know that the pill they are taking does not contain amphetamine, they do not know what these pills do contain. Because many case studies illustrating the dangers of diet aids have been reported, the authorities have seriously considered reclassifying these drugs to make them more difficult to obtain.

DO YOU SLEEP?

INSOMNIA, the great curse of the American people, is the direct result of Nervous Exhaustion, consequent upon Overwork, Worry, and Mental Strain. The common recourse of the sufferer, is to Opium, Morphine, Chloral, Valerian, Phosphorus, and other drugs whose continued use is fatal.

VERVE contains none of these substances. It is purely vegetable, acts directly upon the exhausted nerve centres, and by its tonic action, produces a healthful, natural sleep, with no after effects. Two or three bottles have cured permanently cases of Insomnia, of months' standing. In Neuralgia, Nervous Irritability, Headache, Mental Depression, Hysteria, Loss of Energy following overwork or continued excitement, and all diseases of the Nervous system it is of inestimable value. Merchants and Business men, Clergymen, Lawyers, Authors, and all persons subject to long-continued mental labor, will find natural sleep easily at hand with this remedy in their possession.

A 19th-century magazine advertisement for "Verve," a "purely vegetable" sleeping medicine safer than narcotics. The manufacturer warns that the continued use of drugs like opium and morphine—which were at the time OTC medications—could be fatal.

CHAPTER 5

RELIEF FROM ANXIETY AND INSOMNIA

About one-third of one's life is spent sleeping. A good night's sleep is crucial to good health, emotional stability, and intellectual clarity. Yet, approximately 30% of all people complain about having difficulty falling asleep and/or staying asleep for a normal duration of time. This condition can have a multitude of causes, such as anxiety, stress, depression, excitation, indigestion, or illness. Anxiety can also interfere with one's normal daily activity. Sleeping pills and antianxiety agents may help to alleviate the symptoms of anxiety or insomnia, but if the symptoms continue, the underlying psychological and/or physiological cause(s) should be treated by a professional.

Initially, sleeping pills and antianxiety drugs were relatively easy to obtain with a doctor's prescription. But when scientists and physicians became more aware of the health hazards and high abuse potential of these drugs, the FDA tightened its regulations and doctors changed their prescribing habits. As a result it became more difficult to procure them.

Benzodiazepines (e.g., Valium, Librium) and barbiturates (e.g., Nembutal) are potent relievers of anxiety and insomnia. Prescriptions for Valium and especially barbiturates are more difficult to secure today than they were 10 years ago. From 1971 to 1977 the number of prescriptions for barbiturates decreased from 20 million to only 4 million.

This decline was precipitated by the realization that barbiturates were frequently abused and highly addictive. In fact, barbiturates are often employed by people attempting suicide.

Although the "minor" tranquilizers benzodiazepines and meprobamate (known as Miltown) are safer than the barbiturates, they can cause psychological and physical dependence. In overdose, both the barbiturates and the minor tranquilizers, when taken alone or in conjunction with alcohol, depress brain activity, which can lead to death. As with the barbiturates, after the potential dangers of the minor tranquilizers were more clearly delineated, the total number of prescriptions for them dropped from 90 million in 1977 to 62 million in 1980. Since then there has been a continuous decrease every year. The increasing reluctance of physicians to prescribe these drugs is well founded.

The Misuse of OTC Sleeping Aids

Today there is an enormous demand for sedation and for relief from anxiety and insomnia. Pharmaceutical companies have been quick to promote OTC products that supposedly

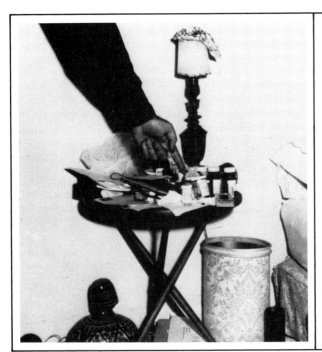

A collection of empty pill bottles on Marilyn Monroe's bedside table. The popular star, who had become increasingly dependent on barbiturates, was found dead of an overdose in August 1962. Most authorities called her death a suicide.

fill this demand. However, after finding that no OTC day-time anxiety reliever or sedative was safe or effective when used for this purpose, in 1979 the FDA published regulations prohibiting the sale of these products.

In reaction, manufacturers quickly repackaged products, such as Compoz and Quiet World, so they could be sold as sleeping aids. To enhance sales, the manufacturers of the leading brands, Nytol, Sominex, and Sleep-Eze, promptly rerouted 60%–70% of their gross income into further promotion of these products. For example, in 1985 the annual advertising budget for Nytol is $3 million. Just listening to the highly suggestive brand names is sleep inducing—for example, Quiet World and Sleep-Eze, or even better, Nytol (G'night y'all) and Allerest (All at rest).

Although the FDA ruled that no OTC drug can be advertised as anxiety reducing, sleeping aids are used, or, more appropriately, are abused for this purpose. For most products marketed as sleeping aids it is difficult to distinguish between those that are really anxiety relievers and those that are actual sleeping aids. This is due partly because

Health experts point out that Americans are among the healthiest people in the world. Pharmaceutical companies, however, spend hundreds of millions of dollars a year to convince consumers that they may have hitherto unsuspected problems, all of which can be easily relieved by the use of "non-habit-forming" drugs.

many consumers believe that a sleeping aid will also relieve daytime anxiety. They understand that too much anxiety, restlessness, or agitation can cause the inability to fall asleep; and since these drugs reduce the nighttime anxiety, they conclude that they also may be used as daytime anxiety relievers. The manufacturer of Tranquil-Span, for example, states outright that this drug "helps calm and relax you," and only indirectly ties this statement to also helping you fall asleep. The name Tranquil-Span itself implies an anxiety-free period of time, and not necessarily sleep. Thus it should not be surprising that these drugs are misused as anxiety relievers.

Antihistamines

Antihistamines, a major ingredient in cold remedies, are also found in sleeping aids. Pyrilamine maleate, diphenhydramine hydrochloride (HCl), and, to a lesser extent, doxylamine succinate are the most common antihistamines used to produce drowsiness. Two of these antihistamines, diphenhydramine HCl and doxylamine succinate, were changed from prescription to nonprescription drugs within the past few years. Some manufacturers also include analgesics such as

A Consumer Products Safety Commission official displays two types of child-resistant drug packaging. The commission recommended them for products containing antihistamines, which can be dangerous if misused.

aspirin or acetaminophen in their sleeping-aid products just in case pain, such as a headache or backache, is a factor causing insomnia.

Although brand names often remain constant over a period of years, the ingredients in any particular brand may change frequently. For example, after the FDA ruled that pyrilamine maleate was unsafe and ineffective as a sleeping aid, Compoz was reformulated to contain the antihistamine diphenhydramine HCl instead. The manufacturer of Sominex, which still contains 25 mg of pyrilamine maleate as the active ingredient, manufactured and packaged Sominex 2, which contains the FDA approved antihistamine diphenhydramine HCl. Both products are now available side by side at your local pharmacy. Nervine also still contains pyrilamine

A typical patent medicine, "Dr. Guertin's Nerve Syrup" promised relief for a wide variety of complaints. Such products enjoyed enormous popularity in the 19th and early 20th centuries. One advertisement contained a sworn testimonial from a customer who said, "I am satisfied that my life has been preserved and my health entirely restored."

maleate. Clearly, manufacturers are not very interested in educating the consumer so that he or she can intelligently evaluate and compare OTC products.

Anticholinergics

Until a few years ago, the anticholinergics scopolamine and atropine were also sold alone or in combination with antihistamines for relief from anxiety and insomnia. They are effective for this purpose because, in addition to drying up runny noses (see Chapter 2), the anticholinergic drugs cause drowsiness and sedation. However, they also cause side effects such as dry mouth, nose, and throat, blurred vision, ringing ears, upset stomach, decreased appetite, and thickened bronchial secretions. Elderly people are likely to experience dizziness and confusion, and men may have trouble in initiating urination, especially if they already have an enlarged prostate gland. At higher doses, nervousness, tremors, muscle spasms, and even convulsions may occur. And

"Synthetic sleep" products available in the 1930s were based on formulas developed in Germany and seized by U.S. authorities after World War I. The principal ingredient in all the preparations was Veronal, the first barbiturate, which had been introduced in 1903.

hallucinations, heart palpitations, headaches, and, paradoxically, insomnia are also not uncommon. Because of the prominence of these undesirable effects, the FDA has prohibited the sale of anticholinergics.

Combination Products

In 1979 it was common to encounter methapyrilene (an antihistamine) and scopolamine (an anticholinergic) in the same sleep aid. Although these drugs are no longer manufactured, people who purchased them previously may still have them in their medicine cabinets.

Unfortunately, once people discovered that these drugs could get you high, they were abused. The synergism (when two drugs together produce effects greater than either one alone) of anticholinergic and antihistaminergic effects, magnified by the ingestion of very high doses, created effects which, though rarely fatal, were not uncommonly associated with drug-induced psychosis. This condition was characterized by hallucinations, confusion, disorientation, delirium, and agitation, or hyperactivity. Drastically increased heart rate (as high as 140 beats per minute), hypertension, and varying degrees of coma are also common effects associated

One does not need to rely on potentially dangerous drugs to treat insomnia. Chamomile tea, made from the flowers of the herb **Anthemis nobilis** is a natural sedative and anxiety reliever. Hot milk, drunk just before going to bed, increases sleep time and decreases nighttime restlessness. And exercise done early in the day dramatically improves sleep.

with the abuse of these substances. A 1977 report in a scientific journal described five deaths that were directly attributable to these products.

Advertising

The sleeping aids that are still being sold have the potential to be dangerous. As mentioned above, they all contain antihistamines, some of which have already been proven to be ineffective and/or unsafe. While these drugs were designed to treat allergic reactions, their use as a sleeping aid is based solely on their side effect of producing drowsiness in some people.

People continue to use these drugs simply because drug companies continue their advertising campaigns. In 1977 Bristol-Myers, one of the largest pharmaceutical companies in the world, spent over $114 million on television ads, while General Motors (the world's largest automobile manufacturing company) spent about $91 million. The drug companies realize that by repeatedly emphasizing a drug's benefits, not only does the consumer come to believe the advertisement, but this belief greatly increases the chances that the product will, in fact, be effective. This placebo effect (see Chapter 7) greatly increases the success of the advertising campaigns, which causes a steady rise in sales.

Saturation advertising techniques are not new, as this view of a London railroad station in 1874 demonstrates. The posters that dominate the space extol the virtues of everything from carpets to baking powder to a medicine that guarantees to cure "headache, biliousness and skin affections."

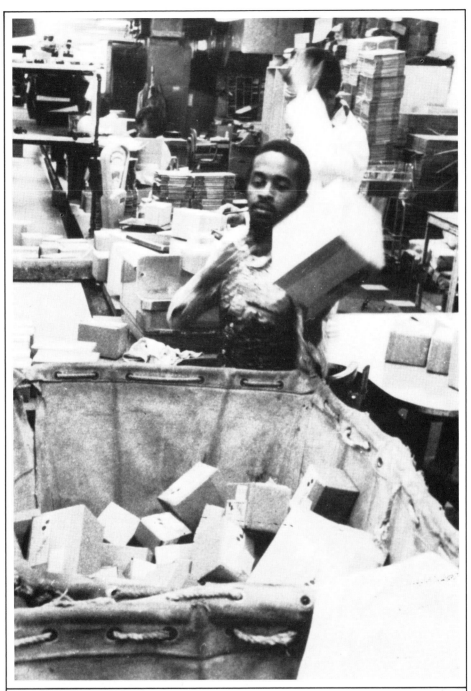

Packages being sorted at a mail-order drug firm. Though statements such as "No sale to minors" or "Items not intended for illegal use" are used in ads, they only serve to make their products more intriguing.

CHAPTER 6

LOOK-ALIKES

Mail-order look-alikes, intended to mimic prescription stimulants and depressants, are numerous and represent a serious problem. For example, there is a look-alike Quaalude (methaqualone) which can be distinguished from the prescription drug only by a very knowledgeable person. Similarly, there are look-alike barbiturates and benzodiazepines (e.g., Valium). In these latter cases the look-alikes contain various combinations of antihistamines, which induce drowsiness.

While the manufacturers of mail-order look-alikes are not always responsible for mimicking prescription drugs (for example, Caffedrine, which is commonly found in drugstores, looks like the prescription amphetamine known on the black market as "Christmas trees"), they are responsible for the majority of health-related problems associated with look-alike drugs. Because look-alikes for prescription depressants are relatively new on the market, and thus there are no available conclusive data, this chapter will deal exclusively with mail-order stimulants.

When one scans the product illustration section in the current Physicians' Desk Reference (PDR), and compares the pictures of prescription stimulants with illustrations in magazines advertising mail-order stimulants, the reason for the term "look-alike" becomes apparent. Even side by side it is difficult to tell the difference between pseudo-speed and the prescription drug.

The existence of look-alikes is not a new phenomenon. For many years illegal dealers of prescription and controlled drugs have diluted or adulterated the original product to increase profits. "Dope pushers" of the 1960s and early 1970s, for example, often diluted amphetamine, mescaline, MDA (methylenedioxyamphetamine, similar to amphetamine and mescaline), and cocaine with baking soda, flour, aspirin, or any other substance without taste and with similar texture and color.

Prescription amphetamine capsules were a popular target for adulteration, since they were unlikely to be opened up for a "taste test." This became especially true after 1970 when Congress passed the Controlled Substances Act, which significantly reduced the availability of amphetamine on the illicit street market. Almost overnight an underground amphetamine industry was born. Because prices had skyrocketed, the prescription amphetamines sold as "uppers" or "pep pills" (as opposed to the powder or crystal form intended

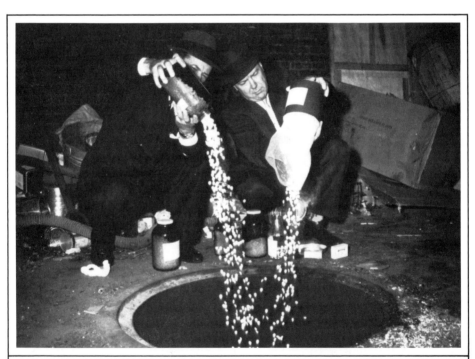

Pennsylvania police officers dump confiscated amphetamine tablets into a Harrisburg incinerator. This action followed the 1970 passage of the Controlled Substances Act, which imposed strict controls on this drug.

for injection) that did reach the streets were usually in capsules so they could be "cut," or adulterated, more easily. Many of the tablets were actually "home pressed," and not even manufactured by a legitimate pharmaceutical company.

The idea behind look-alike stimulants is simple—give the consumer something that looks similar, has a similar effect, and can be bought cheaply. Apparently, at least according to some sources, the present-day situation with look-alikes began with an enterprising truck driver. Following passage of the Controlled Substances Act, Bill Saye realized that he and other long-haul drivers would no longer be able to obtain amphetamines to help them stay awake on their long, cross-country trips. Being business-minded and "concerned" about his fellow truckers, he contacted a New York drug manufacturer. He obtained large quantities of legal OTC diet aids and other caffeine-based stimulants, and

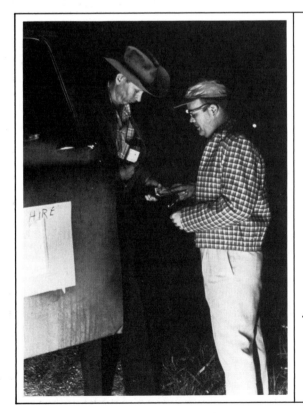

Gathering evidence for an arrest, an undercover federal agent buys amphetamines from a truck driver. Many truckers did a brisk business in "pep pills" after amphetamines had become difficult to obtain legally.

Table 5

Look-Alikes Analysis			
APPROXIMATE DRUG CONTENT RANGE			
DESCRIPTION AND MARKINGS	CAFFEINE (mg)	EPHEDRINE (mg)	PHENYLPRO-PANOLAMINE (mg)
Black and clear capsule, imprinted "18-845," "18-858," "17-875"	100–180	2–25	50
Yellow capsule, imprinted "RJ8," "RUS," "RJS," "18-906"	100–200	25	37–50
Black capsule, imprinted "RJS" ("black beauties"), "DEX," "127"	125–200	25	50
Black capsule, white powder, brown and black granules, imprinted "18-789," "RUS"	44–172	9–25	2–50
Black capsule, white powder, black pellets, imprinted "335"	144–200	25	50–55

SOURCE: *Drug Survival News*, May-June 1981. D I N Publications/Do It Now Foundation.

started selling them from his truck. Before long his CB radio name, "Pea Shooter," became the word also used for the pills he sold. Inadvertently, he began what today is a multi-million dollar business.

Many people quickly realized that there was money to be made. They also remembered the street names of the more popular amphetamine pills. Soon "black beauties," "yellowjackets," "Christmas trees," and "whites" were again available. The ingredients were not as potent, but they were legal.

In 1980 there were 150 registered retailers of look-alikes and about half a dozen mail-order houses. In 1981 alone, sales were approximately $50 million.

The meticulousness with which the new generation of "speed" is manufactured to resemble the old is astounding. It is not only that the size, shape, and color of prescription amphetamine is copied more or less exactly, but even the markings are very similar. Prescription "biphetamine" comes in black capsules marked with a small logo and the numbers 18-875. Certain look-alikes were sold in the same-sized black capsules (thus the name "black beauties"), bearing a slightly different, small logo with the numbers 18-845, 18-858, or

18-789 (see Table 5). The legal counterpart to "Christmas trees" also comes in a transparent green capsule containing white and green grains. The look-alike drug "pink hearts" is intended to mimic prescription dexedrine—they are the same size, and the shape is only slightly different. But as long as there are even barely noticeable differences the mail-order companies are within the law.

Until the end of 1983 most of these legal stimulants contained some combination of caffeine, ephedrine, and PPA. In triple-combination products the highest concentrations of each ingredient were 200 mg of caffeine, 25 mg of ephedrine, and 50 mg of PPA. Both ephedrine and PPA increase blood pressure and heart rate, constrict blood vessels, and, like caffeine, are central nervous system stimulants. Of these three stimulants, PPA has the greatest potential for producing adverse reactions when taken alone. However, PPA is also responsible for increased health risks when taken in combination with certain other prescription drugs, such as antidepressants (e.g., tranylcypromine sulfate or Parnate), antiparkinsonian medications (e.g., methyldopa or Aldomet), and anti-inflammatory drugs (e.g., indomethacin or Indocin). When PPA is used in combination with these drugs, heart rate and blood pressure may be increased to dangerous levels. And if both are combined with PPA, the potential for cardiovascular problems is even further increased.

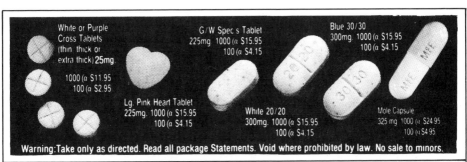

This mail-order drug ad appeared in a magazine in 1985. Typical of such firms, Pocket Rocket Pharmaceutical claimed to be offering "the strongest stimulants available without a prescription." Unknown to many consumers, these drugs, especially when used in combination with other OTC and prescription drugs, can produce many dangerous side effects, including serious cardiovascular problems.

Case Study

A 14-year-old girl was baby-sitting for a neighbor's child. When the girl's mother called to check on things and no one answered the telephone, she went over to see if anything was wrong. She found her daughter on the couch, looking very lethargic and disoriented, and speaking incomprehensibly. Apparently she was complaining about a headache. Her mother called the police and the girl was brought to the hospital, but by the time they arrived she was totally incoherent. Her purse was searched, and pills that looked like amphetamines were found and sent to the lab for analysis.

Meanwhile, the girl's condition worsened, and the whole right side of her body became paralyzed. Initially doctors suspected that she had a brain tumor, but a CAT scan revealed that she had suffered a stroke. A blood test and a chemical analysis of the pills showed that they were look-alike pills—a mixture of PPA, ephedrine, and caffeine. However, it was not known how many pills the girl had taken. Over the next few months the girl's speech improved only slightly, and she had a severe limp and only minimal use of her right arm.

There are many similar reports of strokes associated with these products. There is even one report of a teenager who suffered a stroke after ingesting only one triple-combination pill. Often a dozen or more of these pills are taken at a time, and usually they are "chased" with alcohol.

Look-Alikes in the 1980s

In November 1983 the FDA outlawed all stimulants containing active ingredients other than caffeine. However, the manufacturers were given a few months to sell off their remaining stock.

In a 1984 issue of a popular, drug-oriented publication, there were 10 advertisements for stimulants that could be ordered through the mail. Some even had full-page color ads with pictures of the products. But in all cases the products were referred to in such a way that it was clear that they closely resembled prescription amphetamines. Some ads mentioned ephedrine sulfate as an ingredient. One specified that some of the products were classified by the FDA as bronchodilators. None of the ads mentioned PPA. Look-alike manufacturers can no longer sell combination products, but they can sell PPA, ephedrine, and caffeine separately. Therefore, if a person wants a combination, it is quite easy to purchase them separately and then mix the ingredients.

In 1981 all drug mail-order establishments were located in Pennsylvania. By 1984, however, they had spread to New York, New Jersey, Oregon, Nebraska, Nevada, and Indiana. The wording of their ads has not changed: "stimulants;" "strongest formula available without a prescription;" "safe, legal, no worry." Manufacturers make it seem that there is nothing wrong with taking these legal stimulants, thus it is very difficult to convince people that the drugs used in many of these products can be dangerous. But what if a user is dissatisfied with the effect or the "high"? What is to stop him or her from trying stronger, controlled substances?

During a 1981 hearing before a government committee, a seller of look-alikes testified that he was saving our youth from the ravages of "hard drugs." He said that it was better to take caffeine than amphetamine. And yet, at the same hearing, another witness described the case of a ten-year-old child who had died from an overdose of caffeine.

Various forms of amphetamine. Look-alike stimulants first became popular after the Controlled Substance Act was passed in 1970 and the availability of legal amphetamine was drastically reduced.

"Witches' Sabbath," a 15th-century woodcut. Medieval belief in the supernatural was so powerful that people sometimes fell ill when they believed they had received the curse of a witch.

CHAPTER 7

PLACEBO

Since the beginning of recorded history, flyspecks, snake flesh, mummy powder, asses' hooves, crocodile droppings, and frog sperm have produced many a wondrous cure for even the most stubborn of ailments. One can only speculate on what people may have used as medicine before this time. But as time went on, the physicians' remedies became a trifle more sophisticated. For example, Thomas Jefferson once wrote to a friend that, "One of the most successful physicians I have ever known has assured me that he used more of bread pills, drops of colored water, and powders of hickory ashes than of all other medicines put together."

Most of these concoctions worked because of a phenomenon known as the *placebo effect.* It was first alluded to in published form by Robert Burton in 1628: "An empiric oftentimes, and a silly chirurgeon, doth more strange cures than a rational physician ... because his patient puts his confidence in him." Near the end of the 18th century Benjamin Franklin led a commission to investigate this phenomenon. The commission concluded that the patient's imagination was responsible for the bizarre occurrences, and the unbelievable cures were not a result of mesmerization per se. In fact, contrary to popular belief, no scientific study has furnished conclusive proof that the occurrence of the placebo effect is related to the suggestibility of an individual at all.

One definition of placebo is "a preparation, devoid of pharmacologic effect, given for psychological effect, or as a control in evaluating a medicinal believed to have pharmacologic activity." The word placebo is derived from Latin, meaning "I shall please." And this is exactly what placebos are meant to do.

Because of a patient's trust in his or her doctor placebos may have significant effects. This is no different from trusting a television commercial, a magazine ad, or word of mouth. Once a doctor or a television actor has a person's trust, he or she may be easily convinced of the effectiveness of whatever product is being "sold." The manner in which the medication is given and the setting in which it is administered also contribute to the overall effect. Thus, in effect, watching a television ad in which a very compassionate wife gives her husband a cold remedy, and receiving medicine from your own sympathetic doctor are much the same.

Some OTC products depend on the placebo effect almost exclusively. The FDA has found many drugs sold as OTC products to be entirely ineffective for treatment of the illness for which they are intended. Yet, products that have been shown to have no pharmacological effect are still on the market, and people continue to buy them. Perhaps they know something that the clinical tests have not shown. It is likely that the actual benefits associated with these drugs are due to the placebo effect.

Doctors knowingly use placebos more than most pa-

In the classic 1939 film **The Wizard of Oz,** *the Tin Man got a ticking pocket watch and felt he had a heart; the Cowardly Lion was awarded a medal for courage and became brave; and the Scarecrow was given a diploma and knew he had a brain. All three cases are examples of the placebo effect.*

tients are aware. How does a patient actually know that a drug is working because of its pharmacological action and not its placebo effect? One way to answer this question is to test a drug in a *double-blind* experiment.

Double-Blind Studies

Because the placebo effect can be very strong and is responsible for a significant percentage of a drug's therapeutic efficacy, new pharmacological substances are today routinely tested in double-blind experiments.

A double-blind study compares the efficacy of a drug with that of a placebo. One-half of the patients are given the pharmacologically inert (ineffective) placebo and the other half receive the drug; but neither the doctors, nurses, or patients know who received what until the study is concluded. This is referred to as double-blind because both groups, the patients and the judges, are "blind" as to who receives a drug and who receives a placebo.

Because it has been shown that the doctor's faith in a drug's curative power has a marked effect on the patient's

Cosmas (left) was a 3rd-century physician, and his brother Damian was an apothecary. Christian missionaries and martyrs, they became the patron saints, respectively, of doctors and druggists.

perception of the drug's effectiveness, it is important to ensure that this confidence in the new drug does not influence the results of the study. By keeping the doctor in the dark he or she will treat both the drug and the placebo in the same fashion. And the patient's desire for a favorable outcome from the treatment thereby increases the possibility that *both* placebo and drug are effective. Thus, any positive or negative effects can be attributed only to the action of the drug.

Impure Placebos

Placebos are described as being pure (a sugar pill or a saline injection, both of which have no pharmacologic action) and impure (vitamin B_{12} or penicillin, when used to treat an illness for which they have no effect). Because of vitamin B_{12}'s limited pharmacologic activity and low cost it is probably the most popular placebo prescribed by doctors. In the years 1980 and 1981, of 1.2 billion office visits in the United States, 8 million resulted in a B_{12} prescription for patients who had no symptoms that B_{12} could have affected at all.

Most OTC preparations fall in the impure placebo category. Studies have repeatedly found that impure placebos are generally more successful than pure, or totally inert, substances in producing the suggested subjective effect in the patient. For example, patients who are suffering from anxiety may be given a drug that does affect their physiology (e.g., causes light-headedness, dry mouth, and/or dilated pupils) or one that has no effect at all. If they are told in both cases that they will feel relaxed, it is likely that they will feel more relaxed after taking the drug that has some kind of physiological action. It is possible that any noticeable effects are interpreted by the patient as being related to the desired subjective experience, in this case relaxation. Or perhaps any change in their internal state is perceived as being beneficial.

As long as a drug has some effect its other placebo-type effects will actually amplify the main effect. OTC drugs depend on this phenomenon to a large extent. Antihistamines, apart from blocking inflammation due to histamine release, have a dozen or so other effects. What may be called a side effect when the drug is used for one purpose may be a main effect when the drug is used for another purpose. Advertisements select and focus on the effect they want to be noticed. This is why when advertisers repeatedly state that Sominex and Sleep-Eze aid sleep, there is a good chance they will.

This concept plays a highly important role in the use and abuse of legal, illegal, nonprescription, and prescription drugs. If a teenager's best friend tells him that if he takes two "black beauties" he will get high and feel just great all night long, as long as the drug produces some physiological signs of euphoria his friend's assertions could boost a mild experience to a great high.

Pure Placebos

Pure placebos are also capable of affecting physiology. They may cause changes in blood pressure, heart rate, blood cell counts, creatinine and lipoprotein levels, respiratory rate, pupil size, body temperature, gastrointestinal secretions, and bowel movements. It is surprising what a sugar pill can do if given by the right person and under the proper conditions.

"Wizard Oil" was one of the 19th century's most popular OTC placebos.

The pain-relieving effects of placebos have been the most widely studied and are the most well established. Since the brain does not differentiate between "imagined" pain (that caused by mental events) and "real" pain (that caused by the activation of pain receptors in the body), placebo treatments are just as effective in relieving both types. *Endorphins,* chemicals found in the brain, are now well recognized as the body's own painkillers. They act in the same way as opiates such as morphine or codeine. When one is given a placebo and told it is a very effective pain-killer, endorphins are released and have a significant pain-relieving effect.

Thus, placebos do much more than just make people think they are better. Whenever a person unknowingly ingests an inert placebo when he or she is expecting an effect, 30% to 40% of the time that effect is apt to occur. And sometimes the expected or desired effect is accompanied by the same side effects associated with the ingestion of the pharmacologically active drug. There is no such thing as a harmless drug or a perfectly harmless placebo.

Size, Shape and Color

Studies designed to clarify the relationship between form (capsule or tablet), size, shape, and color of pills have provided some interesting results. In most cases the larger the tablet or capsule, the greater the placebo effect. This is supported by the fact that capsules which are larger than, though pharmacologically equal to, tablets are usually perceived as being stronger than tablets.

Most interesting are recent findings correlating the color of the pill and the anticipated effect. Yellow, orange, and, to some small extent, bright red and black are most often associated with stimulants or antidepressants. On the other hand, white is mostly associated with analgesics and narcotics. This type of information is frequently used by drug manufacturers, both to promote sales and to increase the effectiveness of drugs.

Placebos: Pros and Cons

Many physicians feel that the use of placebos is deceitful and therefore unethical. They argue that they "can heal just as well without deception." They also state that the use of placebos perpetuates quackery, since quacks depend heavily on placebos.

It can be argued that there is nothing wrong with a white lie that persuades the patient to purchase a much less expensive placebo prescription if it has the same effects as a more expensive drug. One cannot ignore the fact that even the strongest drugs have placebo effects that are diminished or enhanced by various stimuli only indirectly related to the drug itself. Most Americans are very drug-oriented and are more likely to opt for a quick medical cure than for a healthier, preventive life style. But clearly, if the supply of placebos and many OTC drugs were to be completely denied to the public, people would be forced to seek alternatives within a new mode of living.

When a doctor prescribes a placebo, he or she hopefully has the patient's best interest in mind. In the case of an advertisement, however, the motivation is more likely to be financial. And yet, the ads are not totally misleading—even placebos are beneficial 30% to 40% of the time. The FDA is struggling with this very fine distinction between deception of and deceit against the public. But as long as people continue to rely heavily on the continued use of these drugs to feel better and to cope with everyday life, OTC products will undoubtedly remain on the market.

Extended-release capsules, with their hundreds of individual grains of medication, are usually perceived as being more potent than tablets, even when they are of equal strength.

In the movie "Popeye," the comic-strip spinach-eating sailor had the right idea. When cooked briefly, spinach is an excellent source of vitamins A, E, K, C, B_1 (thiamine), B_2 (riboflavin), and niacin.

CHAPTER 8

NUTRITIONAL SUPPLEMENTS

Because vitamins are not considered drugs, they can be marketed without FDA control. This alone is probably part of the reason why vitamins and related products outsell every other category of OTC products. In 1981 sales of nutritional products (just less that $2 billion) were more than twice as great as those of the next two highest sellers—analgesics and cold remedies. In 1984 the figures for vitamin sales were far in excess of $2 billion. Americans have been growing increasingly aware of the importance of proper nutrition, partly because of wide coverage by the media, and partly because of the growing realization by the medical profession that a good diet is essential to good health. The old adage "you are what you eat" is probably more true than people ever realized.

With the pace of life ever increasing, many people have become dependent on 10-minute meals so as not to waste too much time. To make sure that our bodies remain capable of functioning more or less normally, we take Alka Selzer to treat indigestion and mega-vitamins to provide the other ingredients our meal may have lacked. Mega-vitamins are pills that contain one or more vitamins in amounts 10 or more times the Recommended Daily Allowance (Table 6).

Popular literature extols the virtues of taking vitamin supplements in mega-doses. The supposed benefits include the prevention of cancer, increased sexual prowess, pre-

Table 6

Recommended Daily Allowances		
NUTRIENT	MALES	FEMALES
Vitamin C (mg)	60	60
Thiamine (mg)	1.4	1.0
Riboflavin (mg)	1.6	1.2
Niacin (mg)	18	13
Vitamin B_6 (mg)	2.2	2.0
Folacin (μg)	400	400
Vitamin B_{12} (μg)	3.0	3.0
Vitamin A (μg)	1000	800
Vitamin D (μg)	5	5
Vitamin E (mg)	10	8

SOURCE: Food and Nutrition Board, National Academy of Sciences, National Research Council Committee on Dietary Allowances, 1980. Recommended for healthy adults ages 23–50. May vary for other age groups, during pregnancy and lactation. Official recommendations for vitamin K, biotin, or pantothenic acid have not been established.

vention or cure of the common cold, retardation of the aging process, increased capability to handle stress, and prevention and cure of mental illness.

Diets centered around multiple vitamins and minerals in mega-doses have been the focus of investigations of practically every type of mental illness. This type of therapy is referred to as *orthomolecular psychiatry*. Most commonly included in such a regimen are niacin, vitamin C, pyridoxine, vitamin E, and vitamin B_{12}. Claims include the cure and even prevention of schizophrenia, neurosis, depression, alcoholism, hyperactivity, and autism. However, these claims do not stand up in double-blind studies.

The term "vitamin" carries with it the connotation of well-being and health. Although vitamins are essential and generally beneficial to our health, many people do not really appreciate their true function. Of the thousands of substances that the human body needs in order to function properly, there are 47 that the human body cannot synthesize from other compounds and thus have to be supplied by the food we eat. Of these 47, 13 are vitamins.

The function of vitamins was first realized around the turn of the century. Ever since vitamins, at least in the public's eye, have been acquiring ever increasing magical powers. Practically all claims of cures or prophylaxis (prevention) are illogically based on the reversal of symptoms accompanying special vitamin deficiencies. For example, vitamin E has been lauded as a veritable guarantor of male virility and sexual prowess. This is based on the fact that vitamin E deficiency causes sterility in male laboratory rats. If these rats are given sufficient amounts of vitamin E within a certain period of time, then the sterility is reversed. To date there is no significant evidence that would corroborate assertions that high vitamin E intake will increase sexual function to above normal levels.

This type of faulty reasoning forms the basis of many arguments put forward by proponents of mega-vitamin therapy. The examples that follow should further clarify this point. Despite the inaccuracy of vitamin-related information, one should keep in mind that compared to all the other substances discussed in this book, vitamins do in fact have the least potential to do any harm. Nonetheless, this is not to say that they can do no harm.

Laboratory rats wait for their daily dose of B_{12}. One gram of B_{12} supplies the daily requirements of 20 million rats, and one-millionth of a gram per day will treat pernicious anemia in humans.

In 1985 the quantities of vitamins being ingested by the general population are more than alarming. The fact that the media is successfully convincing us that eating "alphabet soup" in pill form is beneficial has created a new kind of drug-abuse problem.

Vitamins are most practically divided into water-soluble or fat-soluble. Since the body quickly excretes and does not store water-soluble vitamins, they are virtually harmless. However, because fat-soluble vitamins are stored in fat cells (lipid tissue), and therefore remain in the body for much longer periods of time, they have much greater potential for toxicity.

Water-Soluble Vitamins

Vitamin C, or ascorbic acid, is the most widely renowned water-soluble vitamin. It is also the vitamin most frequently used in mega-doses. Because it is so popular, more is known about its use than any of the other vitamins. Though it has the reputation as a prophylactic and as a cure for the common cold, tests nearly conclusively show that it will not prevent the occurrence of a cold; however, it might decrease the severity and duration of the infection. To achieve this effect, however, the daily mega-doses of 500 mg–2000 mg frequently taken by many individuals are not required. In fact, supplements of even less than 100 mg per day are

An orange picker inspects his crop. Though oranges are the best-known sources of vitamin C, it is also available in such fruits as papayas, strawberries, mangos, and cantaloupes and in such vegetables as tomatos, broccoli, brussel sprouts, and mustard greens.

sufficient. This amount is found in just one glass of orange juice.

Apart from its supposed effect on the common cold, vitamin C has also been asserted to be effective treatment for many viral, bacterial, and fungal infections. There is, however, no reliable evidence for this.

Daily intake of large doses of vitamin C has also been recommended for the prevention of post-transfusion hepatitis (inflammation of the liver), venous thrombosis (clotting of the blood in a vein), some of the complications associated with diabetes mellitus, lung damage from air pollution (including smoking), and sudden infant death. It is also purported to enhance the healing of wounds and to increase alertness, overall mental capability, and the ability to cope with stress. Of these claims very few are substantiated.

There is reason to believe that vitamin C may be beneficial in guarding against venous thrombosis, but evidence is not yet conclusive. The claim that vitamin C is beneficial in the healing of wounds is based on its importance in the formation of *collagen,* a fibrous protein found in bone, cartilage, and connective tissue which is involved in the process of wound healing. Furthermore there is evidence that high vitamin C intake is of therapeutic value in the treatment of corneal burns. However, scientific proof is lacking to support similar wound-healing properties in any other bodily tissues.

Even with massive doses, vitamin C rarely causes adverse reactions. There are exceptions, however. Vitamin C used in excess of 1000 mg per day has been associated with diarrhea, gastrointestinal irritation, and abdominal cramps. Part of this is due to the fact that vitamin C is an acid, hence its name, ascorbic acid. The possibility of forming gallstones (nephrolithiasis) is apparently increased with high doses, especially in individuals already predisposed to this illness.

Whenever any substance is given to an organism in abnormally high amounts, the metabolic processes that utilize that substance are altered—generally accelerated to deal with the increased amounts. If the supply of the substance suddenly returns to the normal level, the metabolic processes for that substance are still set for the previous high level, and the substance is therefore metabolized and excreted at the previous high rate. This results in a net deficiency for that substance.

If mega-doses of vitamin C are suddenly halted the symptoms associated with vitamin C deficiency can occur. The only serious vitamin C withdrawal symptom is scurvy. Scurvy is characterized by weakness, spongy gums, anemia, and bleeding of the mucous membranes. Because pregnant women are made very aware of the fact that the presence or absence of practically anything in their bodies is going to affect their baby, many try to guarantee their baby's health by taking mega-vitamins. Doing this with vitamin C will cause "rebound scurvy" in the newborn, if, after the child is born the mega-doses of vitamin C are no longer made available.

B vitamins are popular because of their alleged role in preventing and alleviating stress-related problems. The B-complex vitamins include thiamine (B_1), riboflavin (B_2), niacin, pyridoxine (B_6), folic acid, B_{12}, pantothenic acid, and biotin. A number of other substances are also frequently commercialized under the B-complex rubric, though they really do not belong there. These include choline, inositol, para-aminobenzoic acid (PABA), orotic acid (B_{13}), pargamic

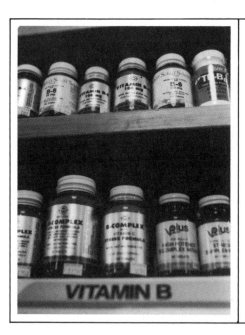

Health-food store shelves are crowded with pills and capsules containing vitamin B complex, which is actually 13 separate vitamins. A well-balanced diet provides most people with adequate B vitamins, but pregnant women, children, and individuals who ingest excessive amounts of carbohydrates may need extra vitamin B.

acid (B_{15}), and laetrile (B_{17}). Some are included because they are growth factors (e.g., choline and inositol); others, such as orotic acid and laetrile, have no basis for inclusion as either growth factors or vitamins. Orotic acid is a coenzyme in the biosynthetic pathway of nucleotides (which are important substances in the formation of DNA and RNA), whereas laetrile includes a group of related organic substances obtained from plants. There is as yet no conclusive evidence that laetrile plays any significant role in animal metabolism or in the cure for cancer (as popularly believed).

Thiamine is supposedly capable of relieving depression, anxiety, and mental illness, as well as preventing senility. It has no known adverse effects when taken orally.

Riboflavin is proclaimed to ensure healthier skin, nails, and hair and to improve vision. It also has no known negative effects.

Niacin, which comes in the form of nicotinic acid or nicotinamide, is associated with significant pharmacologic effects and has therefore been studied quite extensively. Although it is effective as a fat-lowering agent in people suffering from hyperlipemia (an excess of fat or lipids in the blood), it has no weight-reducing effects on people not

Morticia in "The Addams Family" evaluating Uncle Fester's weight loss. For those people who suffer from hyperlipemia, an excess of fat in the blood, niacin has proven to be effective as a fat-lowering agent.

suffering from this disease. There is also no proof that it is beneficial in reducing cholesterol levels. The most common side effects are flushing of the face, neck and chest and cardiac arrhythmias (abnormal heart beats). However, even at relatively low doses (100 mg–300 mg) both nicotinamide and nicotinic acid use can lead to headaches, cramps, nausea, vomiting, diarrhea, hypotension, and hypoglycemia. At higher doses, the major concern is hepatotoxicity.

Vitamin B_6 (pyridoxine, pyridoxal, and pyridoxamine) is of concern because contraceptive-induced abnormalities are reversible with vitamin B_6 supplementation. In addition, a number of cases have been reported in which increased vitamin B_6 intake was effective in alleviating premenstrual tension. However, vitamin B_6 is known to cause dependency at doses as low as 200 mg per day.

Folic acid is relatively less popular. It has been used in the treatment of women with a high risk for neural-tube defects in their children. But again, proof of its positive effects is merely circumstantial. Anecdotal evidence suggests that it may decrease the beneficial effects of phenytoin, a chemical used in the treatment of epileptics. The major concern with folic acid is that it masks vitamin B_{12} deficiency.

The possible role of folic acid in mental disorders has

Soybeans, shown here both shelled and unshelled, are rich in protein and folic acid, a vitamin also abundant in other legumes, such as garbanzos, kidney beans, lima beans, white beans, and peas. Cultivated in China since before 3500 B.C.E., the soybean is a versatile and extremely nutritious vegetable and is 35% protein.

received considerable attention. In several studies institutionalized mental health patients exhibited abnormally low folic acid levels in 20% to 50% of cases. However, subsequent studies prompted by this finding did not show that patients experienced any consistent improvement following folic acid supplementation.

Vitamin B$_{12}$. An adult stores about 5 mg of vitamin B$_{12}$ (mainly in the liver) and only about 1 µg (microgram) daily is required to maintain this level. Since many people ingest as much as 85 mg daily, dietary deficiency of vitamin B$_{12}$ is extremely rare. It can only occur after a prolonged, strict vegetarian diet that excludes all meat, eggs, and dairy products.

One of the few instances in which vitamin B$_{12}$ supplementation is of benefit is in patients suffering from *pernicious anemia,* a disorder that prevents the absorption of B$_{12}$ into the blood stream. When it is given intravenously to replenish B$_{12}$ stores, it characteristically results in short-term acne, usually not lasting longer than one week.

Pantothenic acid has no known pharmacologic effects. One study, using human volunteers, reported that it is helpful in coping with the stress of being immersed in cold water. Even at high doses no interactions with other medications or toxicity have been noted.

Vegetarians have to worry about vitamin B$_{12}$ deficiency, for this vitamin is most abundant in animal products, such as eggs. Tempeh, an Indonesian soy product, is also a good source of vitamin B$_{12}$.

Fat-Soluble Vitamins

Vitamins A, D, E, and K are fat-soluble vitamins. Since they are stored in the fat cells of the body, rather than being rapidly metabolized and excreted, they have a much greater propensity for causing adverse effects than do water-soluble vitamins. Each of them individually may reach different levels at various times (depending on daily intake and rate of metabolism for each of these vitamins in an individual), and thus they can have something analogous to a "seesaw" effect on one another. If low levels of fat-soluble vitamins are generally present, and only one of them is taken in supranormal amounts, its toxicity will be very noticeable and possibly exaggerated. Conversely, if high or adequate levels of a fat-soluble vitamin are present and a person ingests high levels of another one of these vitamins, no adverse symptoms are noted. For example, high vitamin E concentrations protect against both vitamin A and vitamin D toxicity, and high concentrations of vitamin D protect against symptoms of vitamin A deficiency, and vice versa.

Vitamin A is very popular due to a handful of encouraging, albeit misrepresented, reports. Frequently included in popular literature are claims of vitamin A's prevention of cancer, aid in increasing resistance to a wide variety of ailments and diseases (including acne), and promotion of healthy bones, skin, hair, teeth, and gums. Most of these claims are, however, based on very meager, if any, scientific evidence.

Vitamin A is primarily stored in the liver. Therefore, the major concern with both short- and long-term, high-level intake of vitamin A is its hepatotoxicity. In fact, prolonged mega-doses of vitamin A have been known to result in tender bones, hair loss, bleeding, nausea, vomiting, and anorexia. Furthermore, although some current magazine articles claim otherwise, a mega-dose vitamin A intake is definitely not advisable for pregnant mothers. An above-normal incidence of deformations in almost all fetal organ systems has been found to be highly correlated with this type of high vitamin A diets.

Fortunately, in most cases, if normal levels of vitamin A intake are resumed before permanent damage is done, hepa-

Table 7

| Fat-Soluble Vitamins and Their Sources ||
FAT-SOLUBLE VITAMINS	NATURAL SOURCES
Vitamin A Essential for bone formation, healthy skin & mucous membranes.	*Retinol,* found in meat products, and *carotene,* which is found in yellow/orange fruits & vegetables, & leafy green vegetables, including carrots; butternut & hubbard squash; sweet potatoes; cantaloupe; tomatoes; papaya; red peppers; turnip, mustard & beet greens; kale; broccoli.
Vitamin D Essential for bone growth, metabolism of calcium & phosphorous.	Sunshine, eggs, milk & other dairy products.
Vitamin E May counteract respiratory problems caused by air pollution.	Vegetable oils, especially wheat germ, walnut, sunflower & safflower oil; sunflower seeds, almonds, hazelnuts & walnuts; spinach, sweet potatoes, beet & turnip greens.
Vitamin K Necessary for normal clotting of blood.	Leafy green vegetables, egg yolk, soybean oil.

All vitamins occur naturally in foods and are essential for bodily functions. In a recent report, the American Cancer Society claimed that "foods rich in carotene or vitamin A may lower the risk of cancer."

totoxic reactions associated with high vitamin A levels are reversible.

Vitamin D is probably the least abused vitamin. Because it is known to be extremely toxic, even the lay literature does not promote its use. Its potential for toxicity is almost exclusively rooted in its very prominent role as a regulator of calcium metabolism. It is intimately involved in transporting calcium across the intestinal wall. Abnormally high vitamin D levels cause hypercalcemia—abnormally elevated levels of calcium. This is often characterized by weakness, increased urination, thirst, nausea, anorexia, sleepiness, and/or stupor.

In one case a young boy had been ingesting as much as 250,000 IU (international units) of vitamin A and 4000 IU of vitamin D per day. Finally he suffered from excessive amounts of calcium in the blood, increased intracranial pressure, headaches, rash, fever, swelling of face and limbs due to fluid retention, bone pain and tenderness, and other

Pennsylvania governor Dick Thornburgh drinks to the adoption of milk as the official beverage of his state, one of the nation's major milk producers. Milk is a superior source of complete protein, as well as of calcium, riboflavin, and vitamin D, which is usually added after the milk has been pasteurized.

symptoms. Fortunately, he recovered after hospitalization.

Children are much more prone to the toxic effects of both vitamin A and D, while adults are relatively resistant. Although daily doses of 10,000 IU per day have resulted in complications after only a few months, usually doses of 50,000 IU–500,000 IU daily over a period of years are required to produce adverse effects in adults.

Vitamin E is probably the next most popular vitamin after vitamin C. It has been marketed and widely sold as a restorer or enhancer of male virility. It is also renowned as a prophylactic and cure for a variety of skin problems. In this area it is credited with speeding up the healing process of nearly any kind of superficial wound, as well as being able to create a healthy skin tone. There is reliable scientific data that conclusively supports these claims. Vitamin E has also been widely acclaimed as a cure for fibrocystic breast disease, an abnormal increase of fibrous connective tissue in the breast. Again, no conclusive data is available.

Rudolph Valentino (1895–1926) demonstrates the passionate look that made him the 1920s' best-known male sex symbol. The silent-film star was said to use aphrodisiacs in an effort to boost his sexual powers.

Ever since 1946, when vitamin E gained a reputation as being useful in treating angina pectoris (recurrent pain in the chest and left arm caused by a sudden decrease of the blood supply to the heart), rumors of its curative powers have increased. Now they include prevention and treatment of many heart-related problems, including myocardial infarctions, rheumatic heart disease, congenital heart disease, and congestive heart failure. However, mega-doses of vitamin E have not yet been proven to have therapeutic value in any type of cardiovascular disorder.

In 1985 vitamin E is still acclaimed as a virtual guarantee for a normal pregnancy. This claim, however, is based on individual cases from the 1940s and 1950s, when women known to spontaneously abort were given mega-vitamin E treatment. Even in these cases the improvement was only marginal and not statistically significant.

Vitamin E has been shown to relieve pain and limping due to peripheral vascular occlusion (i.e., the closing of superficial blood vessels, usually those supplying the leg muscles). And its possible prophylactic effects on athero-

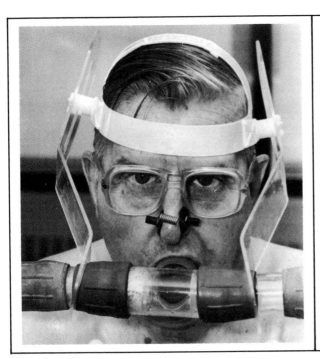

Wearing a nose clamp and a mouthpiece that analyzes his exhaled breath as he exercises, a volunteer takes part in an experiment at Boston's Human Nutrition Research Center on Aging. The project was part of a study aimed at learning how diet and vitamin intake affect the aging process.

sclerosis (a degenerative disease of the arteries) have been noted. Apparently vitamin E redistributes cholesterol stores in such a way that high concentrations of cholesterol in a limited area become unlikely, and therefore the chances of developing atherosclerosis are minimized.

There are also claims of vitamin E preventing thrombophlebitis (inflammation of a vein associated with, or due to, a thrombus, or a blood clot). In fact, most of the above-mentioned claims are conjectural, and based mostly on scattered reports of individual cases and on unreplicated studies. The possibility does exist that in the future some of these effects will be supported by substantial evidence.

Modern-day living exposes us to higher than normal amounts of ozone, nitrogen oxide, and a wide variety of other air pollutants. Vitamin E has, in fact, shown some efficacy in ameliorating respiratory problems associated with this situation.

In a 1974 study, 82% of sufferers of nocturnal leg cramps (50% of which had experienced the symptom for more than five years) benefited from doses of vitamin E.

A thermal inversion, or layer of warm air that traps polluted air beneath it, hovers over Los Angeles. Some medical researchers believe that vitamin E can ease respiratory problems caused by such conditions.

Although vitamin E, being a fat-soluble vitamin, remains in the body for prolonged periods of time, very large daily amounts have rarely been the cause of health problems. Nevertheless, there have been reports of skin eruptions, muscle weakness, and stomach ache associated with daily mega-doses (100 IU–1000 IU) of vitamin E.

Vitamin K, an essential agent involved in blood coagulation, is easily obtained in effective amounts from a more or less normal diet. No serious side effects attributable to mega-doses of vitamin K have as yet been reported.

Because vitamins and other essential nutrients, due to their relatively benign pharmacologic and toxic effects, have traditionally been viewed as undeserving of serious consideration, we in fact know relatively little about them. Therefore, all claims, even those backed by some scientific evidence, should be taken lightly.

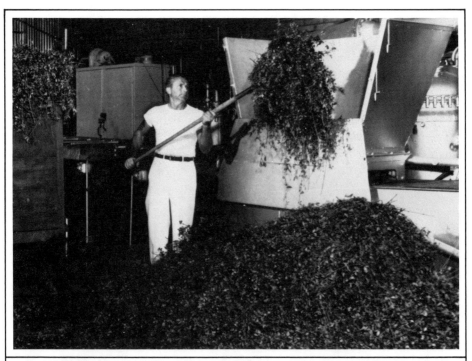

Some nutritional supplements are made from chemical compounds, others from natural ingredients. Here, a worker forks fresh alfalfa into a hopper, where it will be washed, dehydrated, and pressed into tablets.

Vitamins and Cancer

Vitamins A, C, and E are often mentioned in connection with cancer. The association of cancer with low levels of vitamin A have been reported in an appreciable number of studies. One study showed that for at least 12 months prior to the diagnosis of cancer, vitamin A levels were significantly reduced. Remarkable findings such as these recently prompted the American Cancer Society to publish dietary guidelines that recommended consumption of foods high in vitamin A and related carotenoids (chemicals similar to vitamin A in structure and effect). These are highly concentrated in carrots, tomatoes, broccoli, and other yellow and dark-green vegetables.

In animal studies, vitamin A has been shown to provide some degree of protection against the effects of carcinogens, and to postpone or even prevent the development of carci-

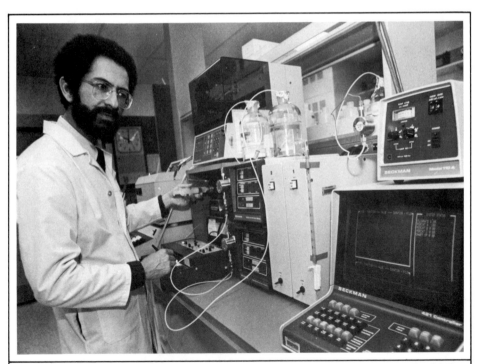

A Tufts University medical researcher demonstrates the operation of a high-performance liquid chromatograph, a device capable of analyzing the way different vitamins affect the body at different ages.

nomas. Unfortunately, the amounts of vitamin A required to be effective (100,000 IU–150,000 IU daily) are also toxic. Other studies have shown no differences in vitamin A and the carotenoid levels between groups of subjects who developed cancer and those who did not.

Vitamins C and E have also been advocated as prophylactics against cancer, based on the finding that both can prevent or at least delay the formation of carcinomas. They inhibit oxidation, and are therefore specifically suited to prevent the development of cancer-causing nitrosamines in the gut. The incidence of gastrointestinal cancer is highly correlated with the formation of nitrosamines; consequently both vitamins have the potential to help reduce its occurrence.

Spurred by such reports, certain proponents of megavitamin therapy have been encouraging the use of very

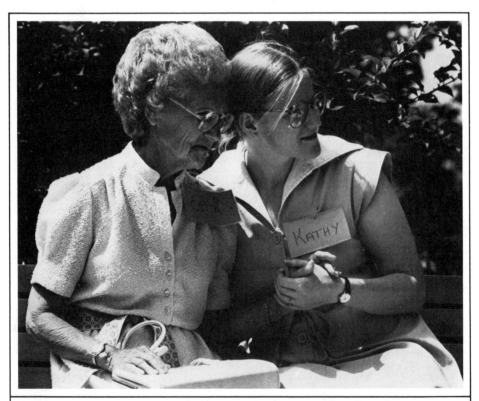

A social worker assists an Alzheimer's disease patient at a community outing. Initial findings show that lecithin and choline alleviate some of the symptoms associated with this disease, though no cure exists.

large amounts of these vitamins, such as daily doses of 10 gm–30 gm of vitamin C for prevention. All in all, more evidence is still required before a final, conclusive statement can be made regarding mega-vitamin treatment as an effective prophylactic against cancer.

Lecithin and Choline

Much is being made of the initial favorable reports of the effects of lecithin and choline on Alzheimer's disease (AD) patients. Present in Alzheimer's disease is a dysfunction (specifically a decreased function) of the cholinergic system (i.e., the neurons and nerves that utilize the neurotransmitter acetylcholine [ACh]). When choline is given to these patients, the body converts it to ACh, and some of the symptoms associated with this disease are alleviated to a certain extent.

Lecithin is simply a large organic molecule known as a *phospholipid* that contains the choline molecule. So the ingestion of either choline or lecithin produces the same effects in the brain and body. Both substances produce some modest, but short-lived improvement in the behavior of AD patients.

These encouraging findings have been used by certain companies to popularize lecithin and choline as "wonder drugs" capable of producing significant improvements in a healthy person's memory. Furthermore they are lauded as being effective protectors against other types of degenerative dementias. Again, more evidence is needed to substantiate these claims.

Monosodium Glutamate and the Chinese Restaurant Syndrome

In 1968 a Chinese physician named Robert Ho Man Kwok arrived in the United States. He had been told that there were many Chinese restaurants in America, and was very pleased when he discovered that there were even more than he had suspected. His initial enthusiasm was soon dampened—whenever he ate in one he became ill. He usually experienced burning, tightness, and numbness in his upper arms, chest, neck, and face. This would start soon after he began dining, and sometimes these symptoms would persist for up to 4 hours.

Dr. Kwok was not the only one who suffered from the Chinese Restaurant Syndrome (CRS). Apparently, anywhere from 2% to 25% of the population (depending on from which study the figures are taken) is prone to this phenomenon. In some people, dining in a Chinese restaurant has also been associated with headaches, dizziness, palpitation, general weakness, nausea, and vomiting. According to the latest data, headache and nausea seem to be the most common symptoms of CRS, which is primarily caused by the ingestion of monosodium glutamate, or MSG (the salt form of the amino acid glutamic acid).

Cooks in the Far East have used the seaweed *Laminaria japonica* as a flavor enhancer for many years. In 1908 it was discovered that MSG was the substance responsible for the flavor enhancement. With this discovery began the commercial production of MSG throughout the world. In 1984 the worldwide MSG industry produced approximately 300,000 tons per year, and each year Americans use about 20,000 tons. MSG production and marketing is controlled only by supply and demand. In general MSG must be listed with the ingredients of packaged foods, though for some reason packages of fresh chicken, mayonnaise, and salad dressing are not required to list it. MSG is also used extensively as a meat tenderizer, such as in the product Accent.

The initial 1968 report by Dr. Kwok prompted much research into the exact nature and causes of the CRS. Based on the first wave of studies, it was believed that in those people sensitive to MSG, less than 3 gm were needed to produce the characteristic syndrome. It was also shown that even nonsusceptible individuals would manifest the characteristic symptoms if given sufficiently high levels of MSG.

Certain methodological hurdles have, however, been encountered with even the most rigorously controlled double-blind studies. The main problem is that people who are prone to the more uncomfortable effects of MSG are also able to detect its taste, no matter how well concealed it seems to be. Even people who are not prone to its negative effects have been known to discern its unique taste no matter in what type of food it is concealed. Thus in this case the double-blind design fails.

Restaurants in San Francisco's Chinatown (above) and other U.S. cities contribute to the annual national use of about 20,000 tons of monosodium glutamate, or MSG, a flavor enhancer with serious side effects.

An unhappy headache-sufferer ingests a bitter-tasting "physic" in a cartoon published in 1800. People have used medicine to purge themselves of their aches and pains since before recorded history.

CHAPTER 9

"DO I REALLY NEED THIS?"

Sometime in the near future you will go to the medicine cabinet in search of an OTC product for one ailment or another. And the chances are very good that this drug will provide some relief. Yet, many of these OTC products are not considered safe and effective for the disorders for which they are usually intended. What if you used a product not considered effective, but insisted that it gave relief? Aside from the placebo effect, whereby one obtains relief only because the desire and belief that the drug will provide it is strong, there are two other reasons why people often get better when taking OTC drugs.

> *First, most of the diseases for which self-medication is appropriate are so-called self-limiting diseases, like the cold, which get better no matter what you do. Second, many of the products with ingredients lacking evidence of effectiveness do have at least one effective ingredient. So if your symptoms respond quickly, even sooner than if the problem ran its natural course, it is probably due to that ingredient, such as aspirin or acetaminophen in a multiple ingredient pain-relief product. The other, ineffective ingredients are not only costing you additional money but are also exposing you to unneeded risks.*
>
> from *Over the Counter Pills that Don't Work*

It is this "additional money" for the pharmaceutical industry which helps keep the products that contain unproven ingredients on the OTC market. Without these ingredients on the market there would be fewer OTC products, and profits would be diminished for the drug industry. If a person were to shop wisely, money could be saved and potential health risks could be decreased. When looking for an OTC product, decide on the most effective ingredient and purchase the product in generic form.

Before you reach for an OTC drug, however, ask yourself this question first: "Do I really need this?" Many symptoms, such as coughs or runny noses, are important in the body's defense against diseases such as the common cold or flu. If the discomfort is not unbearable, it is possible the problem will go away more quickly without the drug. Learn how the body works and how you can help your body heal itself without drugs. Should you decide to take an OTC product, remember that even though it is available without a prescription or the advice of a physician, it can be dangerous. Whether you purchased it from a pharmacy, through a magazine advertisement, or from a friend, it should be used only when needed and with caution.

Scott Nearing, author of **Living the Good Life,** *lived with his wife in rural Maine, where they grew all their food and bartered for those commodities they were unable to produce. Eating organically grown foods and getting regular physical exercise, he avoided all medicines and doctors and remained healthy until he died in 1984, two weeks before his 100th birthday.*

APPENDIX

STATE AGENCIES FOR THE PREVENTION AND TREATMENT OF DRUG ABUSE

ALABAMA
Department of Mental Health
Division of Mental Illness and
  Substance Abuse Community
  Programs
200 Interstate Park Drive
P.O. Box 3710
Montgomery, AL 36193
(205) 271-9253

ALASKA
Department of Health and Social
  Services
Office of Alcoholism and Drug
  Abuse
Pouch H-05-F
Juneau, AK 99811
(907) 586-6201

ARIZONA
Department of Health Services
Division of Behavioral Health
  Services
Bureau of Community Services
Alcohol Abuse and Alcoholism
  Section
2500 East Van Buren
Phoenix, AZ 85008
(602) 255-1238

Department of Health Services
Division of Behavioral Health
  Services
Bureau of Community Services
Drug Abuse Section
2500 East Van Buren
Phoenix, AZ 85008
(602) 255-1240

ARKANSAS
Department of Human Services
Office on Alcohol and Drug Abuse
  Prevention
1515 West 7th Avenue
Suite 310
Little Rock, AR 72202
(501) 371-2603

CALIFORNIA
Department of Alcohol and Drug
  Abuse
111 Capitol Mall
Sacramento, CA 95814
(916) 445-1940

COLORADO
Department of Health
Alcohol and Drug Abuse Division
4210 East 11th Avenue
Denver, CO 80220
(303) 320-6137

CONNECTICUT
Alcohol and Drug Abuse
  Commission
999 Asylum Avenue
3rd Floor
Hartford, CT 06105
(203) 566-4145

DELAWARE
Division of Mental Health
Bureau of Alcoholism and Drug
  Abuse
1901 North Dupont Highway
Newcastle, DE 19720
(302) 421-6101

DISTRICT OF COLUMBIA
Department of Human Services
Office of Health Planning and
  Development
601 Indiana Avenue, NW
Suite 500
Washington, D.C. 20004
(202) 724-5641

FLORIDA
Department of Health and
  Rehabilitative Services
Alcoholic Rehabilitation Program
1317 Winewood Boulevard
Room 187A
Tallahassee, FL 32301
(904) 488-0396

Department of Health and
  Rehabilitative Services
Drug Abuse Program
1317 Winewood Boulevard
Building 6, Room 155
Tallahassee, FL 32301
(904) 488-0900

GEORGIA
Department of Human Resources
Division of Mental Health and
  Mental Retardation
Alcohol and Drug Section
618 Ponce De Leon Avenue, NE
Atlanta, GA 30365-2101
(404) 894-4785

HAWAII
Department of Health
Mental Health Division
Alcohol and Drug Abuse Branch
1250 Punch Bowl Street
P.O. Box 3378
Honolulu, HI 96801
(808) 548-4280

IDAHO
Department of Health and Welfare
Bureau of Preventive Medicine
Substance Abuse Section
450 West State
Boise, ID 83720
(208) 334-4368

ILLINOIS
Department of Mental Health and
  Developmental Disabilities
Division of Alcoholism
160 North La Salle Street
Room 1500
Chicago, IL 60601
(312) 793-2907

Illinois Dangerous Drugs
  Commission
300 North State Street
Suite 1500
Chicago, IL 60610
(312) 822-9860

INDIANA
Department of Mental Health
Division of Addiction Services
429 North Pennsylvania Street
Indianapolis, IN 46204
(317) 232-7816

IOWA
Department of Substance Abuse
505 5th Avenue
Insurance Exchange Building
Suite 202
Des Moines, IA 50319
(515) 281-3641

KANSAS
Department of Social Rehabilitation
Alcohol and Drug Abuse Services
2700 West 6th Street
Biddle Building
Topeka, KS 66606
(913) 296-3925

KENTUCKY
Cabinet for Human Resources
Department of Health Services
Substance Abuse Branch
275 East Main Street
Frankfort, KY 40601
(502) 564-2880

LOUISIANA
Department of Health and Human
  Resources
Office of Mental Health and
  Substance Abuse
655 North 5th Street
P.O. Box 4049
Baton Rouge, LA 70821
(504) 342-2565

MAINE
Department of Human Services
Office of Alcoholism and Drug
  Abuse Prevention
Bureau of Rehabilitation
32 Winthrop Street
Augusta, ME 04330
(207) 289-2781

MARYLAND
Alcoholism Control Administration
201 West Preston Street
Fourth Floor
Baltimore, MD 21201
(301) 383-2977

State Health Department
Drug Abuse Administration
201 West Preston Street
Baltimore, MD 21201
(301) 383-3312

MASSACHUSETTS
Department of Public Health
Division of Alcoholism
755 Boylston Street
Sixth Floor
Boston, MA 02116
(617) 727-1960

Department of Public Health
Division of Drug Rehabilitation
600 Washington Street
Boston, MA 02114
(617) 727-8617

MICHIGAN
Department of Public Health
Office of Substance Abuse Services
3500 North Logan Street
P.O. Box 30035
Lansing, MI 48909
(517) 373-8603

MINNESOTA
Department of Public Welfare
Chemical Dependency Program
  Division
Centennial Building
658 Cedar Street
4th Floor
Saint Paul, MN 55155
(612) 296-4614

MISSISSIPPI
Department of Mental Health
Division of Alcohol and Drug Abuse
1102 Robert E. Lee Building
Jackson, MS 39201
(601) 359-1297

MISSOURI
Department of Mental Health
Division of Alcoholism and Drug
  Abuse
2002 Missouri Boulevard
P.O. Box 687
Jefferson City, MO 65102
(314) 751-4942

MONTANA
Department of Institutions
Alcohol and Drug Abuse Division
1539 11th Avenue
Helena, MT 59620
(406) 449-2827

NEBRASKA
Department of Public Institutions
Division of Alcoholism and Drug Abuse
801 West Van Dorn Street
P.O. Box 94728
Lincoln, NB 68509
(402) 471-2851, Ext. 415

NEVADA
Department of Human Resources
Bureau of Alcohol and Drug Abuse
505 East King Street
Carson City, NV 89710
(702) 885-4790

NEW HAMPSHIRE
Department of Health and Welfare
Office of Alcohol and Drug Abuse
  Prevention
Hazen Drive
Health and Welfare Building
Concord, NH 03301
(603) 271-4627

NEW JERSEY
Department of Health
Division of Alcoholism
129 East Hanover Street CN 362
Trenton, NJ 08625
(609) 292-8949

Department of Health
Division of Narcotic and Drug Abuse
  Control
129 East Hanover Street CN 362
Trenton, NJ 08625
(609) 292-8949

NEW MEXICO
Health and Environment Department
Behavioral Services Division
Substance Abuse Bureau
725 Saint Michaels Drive
P.O. Box 968
Santa Fe, NM 87503
(505) 984-0020, Ext. 304

NEW YORK
Division of Alcoholism and Alcohol
  Abuse
194 Washington Avenue
Albany, NY 12210
(518) 474-5417

Division of Substance Abuse
  Services
Executive Park South
Box 8200
Albany, NY 12203
(518) 457-7629

NORTH CAROLINA
Department of Human Resources
Division of Mental Health, Mental
  Retardation and Substance Abuse
  Services
Alcohol and Drug Abuse Services
325 North Salisbury Street
Albemarle Building
Raleigh, NC 27611
(919) 733-4670

NORTH DAKOTA
Department of Human Services
Division of Alcoholism and Drug
  Abuse
State Capitol Building
Bismarck, ND 58505
(701) 224-2767

OHIO
Department of Health
Division of Alcoholism
246 North High Street
P.O. Box 118
Columbus, OH 43216
(614) 466-3543

Department of Mental Health
Bureau of Drug Abuse
65 South Front Street
Columbus, OH 43215
(614) 466-9023

OKLAHOMA
Department of Mental Health
Alcohol and Drug Programs
4545 North Lincoln Boulevard
Suite 100 East Terrace
P.O. Box 53277
Oklahoma City, OK 73152
(405) 521-0044

OREGON
Department of Human Resources
Mental Health Division
Office of Programs for Alcohol and
   Drug Problems
2575 Bittern Street, NE
Salem, OR 97310
(503) 378-2163

PENNSYLVANIA
Department of Health
Office of Drug and Alcohol
   Programs
Commonwealth and Forster Avenues
Health and Welfare Building
P.O. Box 90
Harrisburg, PA 17108
(717) 787-9857

RHODE ISLAND
Department of Mental Health,
   Mental Retardation and Hospitals
Division of Substance Abuse
Substance Abuse Administration
   Building
Cranston, RI 02920
(401) 464-2091

SOUTH CAROLINA
Commission on Alcohol and Drug
   Abuse
3700 Forest Drive
Columbia, SC 29204
(803) 758-2521

SOUTH DAKOTA
Department of Health
Division of Alcohol and Drug Abuse
523 East Capitol, Joe Foss Building
Pierre, SD 57501
(605) 773-4806

TENNESSEE
Department of Mental Health and
   Mental Retardation
Alcohol and Drug Abuse Services
505 Deaderick Street
James K. Polk Building, Fourth Floor
Nashville, TN 37219
(615) 741-1921

TEXAS
Commission on Alcoholism
809 Sam Houston State Office Building
Austin, TX 78701
(512) 475-2577

Department of Community Affairs
Drug Abuse Prevention Division
2015 South Interstate Highway 35
P.O. Box 13166
Austin, TX 78711
(512) 443-4100

UTAH
Department of Social Services
Division of Alcoholism and Drugs
150 West North Temple
Suite 350
P.O. Box 2500
Salt Lake City, UT 84110
(801) 533-6532

VERMONT
Agency of Human Services
Department of Social and
   Rehabilitation Services
Alcohol and Drug Abuse Division
103 South Main Street
Waterbury, VT 05676
(802) 241-2170

VIRGINIA
Department of Mental Health and
  Mental Retardation
Division of Substance Abuse
109 Governor Street
P.O. Box 1797
Richmond, VA 23214
(804) 786-5313

WASHINGTON
Department of Social and Health
  Service
Bureau of Alcohol and Substance
  Abuse
Office Building—44 W
Olympia, WA 98504
(206) 753-5866

WEST VIRGINIA
Department of Health
Office of Behavioral Health Services
Division on Alcoholism and Drug
  Abuse
1800 Washington Street East
Building 3 Room 451
Charleston, WV 25305
(304) 348-2276

WISCONSIN
Department of Health and Social
  Services
Division of Community Services
Bureau of Community Programs
Alcohol and Other Drug Abuse
  Program Office
1 West Wilson Street
P.O. Box 7851
Madison, WI 53707
(608) 266-2717

WYOMING
Alcohol and Drug Abuse Programs
Hathaway Building
Cheyenne, WY 82002
(307) 777-7115, Ext. 7118

GUAM
Mental Health & Substance Abuse
  Agency
P.O. Box 20999
Guam 96921

PUERTO RICO
Department of Addiction Control
  Services
Alcohol Abuse Programs
P.O. Box B-Y Rio Piedras Station
Rio Piedras, PR 00928
(809) 763-5014

Department of Addiction Control
  Services
Drug Abuse Programs
P.O. Box B-Y Rio Piedras Station
Rio Piedras, PR 00928
(809) 764-8140

VIRGIN ISLANDS
Division of Mental Health,
  Alcoholism & Drug Dependency
  Services
P.O. Box 7329
Saint Thomas, Virgin Islands 00801
(809) 774-7265

AMERICAN SAMOA
LBJ Tropical Medical Center
Department of Mental Health Clinic
Pago Pago, American Samoa 96799

TRUST TERRITORIES
Director of Health Services
Office of the High Commissioner
Saipan, Trust Territories 96950

Further Reading

Alhadeff, L., Gualtieri, T., and Lipton, M. "Toxic effects of water-soluble vitamins." *Nutrition Reviews* vol. 42 (1984): pp. 33–40.

Allen, D.M., Greenblatt, D.J., and Noel, B.J. "Self-poisoning with over-the-counter hypnotics." *Clinical Toxicology* vol. 15 (1979): pp. 151–158.

Beaver, W.T. "Caffeine revisited." *Journal of the American Medical Association* vol. 251 (1984): pp. 1732–1733.

Benowicz, Robert J. *Non-Prescription Drugs & Their Side Effects.* New York: Putnam Publishing Group, 1983.

Blum, A. "Phenylpropanolamine: An over-the-counter amphetamine?" *Journal of the American Medical Association* vol. 245 (1981): pp. 1346–1347.

Cawood, F.W. and Smith, D.C. *Vitamin Side Effects Revealed.* Peachtree City, Georgia: F.C. and A. Publishing, 1984.

Dougherty, R.J. "Pseudo-speed: look-alikes or pea-shooters." *New York State Journal of Medicine* vol. 82 (1982): pp. 74–75.

Esmay, J.B. and Wertheimer, A.I. "A review of over-the-counter drug therapy." *Journal of Community Health* vol. 5 (1979): pp. 54–66.

Griffith, H. Winter. *Complete Guide to Prescription & Non-Prescription Drugs.* Tucson: HPBooks, 1985.

Kaufman, J., Rabinowitz-Dagi, L., Levin, J., McCarthy, P., Wolfe, S., Bargmann, E., and The Public Citizen Health Research Group. *Over-the-Counter Pills that Don't Work.* New York: Pantheon, 1983.

Ritter, R.M. "PPA: diet drug under fire." *Psychology Today* vol. 18 (1984): pp. 8–12.

Vener, A.M., Krupka, L.R., and Climo, J.J. "Drugs (prescription, over-the-counter, social) and the young adult: use and attitudes." *The International Journal of Addiction* vol. 17 (1982): pp. 399–415.

Woolliscroft, J.O. "Megavitamins: fact and fancy." *Disease-A-Month* vol. 29 (1983): pp. 1–56.

Glossary

acetaminophen   N-acetylpara-amino-phenol, or APAP; a potent analgesic and antipyretic chemically similar to aspirin yet without anti-inflammatory action

acetylsalicylic acid   aspirin; an analgesic and antipyretic

addiction   a condition caused by repeated drug use, including a compulsive urge to continue using the drug, a tendency to increase the dosage, and physiological and/or psychological dependence

adenosine   a neurotransmitter affected by caffeine

adjuvant   a drug used to enhance the effects of another drug

adrenal gland   a gland located near the kidney that produces the hormone adrenaline (also known as epinephrine) used in the treatment of asthma

adulterate   to dilute a drug either with an inert material to add bulk or another drug to alter the effects of the original drug

alkaloid   any chemical containing nitrogen, carbon, hydrogen, and oxygen, usually occurring in plants

allergic response   the body's reaction to infected, damaged, or disturbed tissue, characterized by inflammation, sneezing, congestion, runny nose and/or watery, itchy, red eyes

Alzheimer's disease   a dysfunction (specifically a decreased function) of the cholinergic system, characterized by a loss of memory and/or judgment and often accompanied by confusion

analgesic   a drug that produces an insensitivity to pain without loss of consciousness

anorectic   an appetite suppressant

anticholinergic   a drug that alters the normal communication between neurons by binding to the receptor sites normally used by the neurotransmitter acetylcholine (ACh)

antihistamine   a drug that inhibits the action of histamine and thus reduces the allergic response

anti-inflammatory   a drug that reduces inflammation

antipyretic   a drug that reduces fever

antitussive   substances that act to inhibit an uncontrollable, dry, or unproductive cough

aspirin   acetylsalicylic acid; an analgesic, antipyretic, and anti-inflammatory agent originally derived from plants

asthma   a condition characterized by a difficulty in breathing, often caused by constriction of the bronchi of the lungs and treated with epinephrine-related drugs

atherosclerosis   a degenerative disease of the arteries

atropine   an anticholinergic drug extracted from the belladona plant and used to relieve spasms, to diminish secretions, to relieve pain, and to dilate the pupil

autism   a psychological condition characterized by mental activity which is controlled by the wishes of the individual as opposed to mental activity controlled by the conditions imposed by the nature of objects and events

axon   the part of a neuron along which the nerve impulse travels away from the cell body

barbiturate   a drug that causes depression of the central nervous system, generally used to reduce anxiety or to induce euphoria

belladonna   the deadly nightshade; a plant from which many anticholinergics are derived

benzodiazepine   a potent reliever of anxiety and insomnia; includes Valium and Librium

"black beauties"   black-market amphetamines

bronchodilator   a substance that, by dilating the bronchi of the lungs, clears the air passages and aids breathing

buffer   a substance that lowers acidity; sometimes added to aspirin to decrease this drug's irritation to the stomach

caffeine   trimethylxanthine; a central nervous system stimulator found in coffee, tea, cocoa, various soft drinks, and often in combination with other drugs to enhance their effects

carcinogen   a substance that causes the formation of carcinomas which lead to cancer

cardiac arrhythmias   irregular beating of the heart

cataract   a clouding of the lens of the eye

catecholamines neurotransmitters such as epinephrine and dopamine

CAT scan an x-ray technique that produces x-ray photographs of a part of the body from any cross-section or angle

cholinergic system the neurons and nerves that utilize the neurotransmitter acetylcholine (ACh)

codeine a sedative and pain-relieving agent found in opium and related to morphine but less potent

coenzyme a nonprotein compound that forms the active portion of an enzyme system

collagen a fibrous protein found in bone, cartilage, and connective tissue and involved in the process of healing

dendrites hair-like structures protruding from the neural cell body on which receptor sites are located

dextromethorphan an antitussive

diabetes mellitus a disorder caused by an inadequate secretion or utilization of insulin and characterized by thirst, hunger, itching, weakness, loss of weight, and, when severe, coma

dilation the action of stretching or expanding an organ or part of the body

DNA deoxyribonucleic acid; the substance found in the cell nucleus and associated with the transmission of genetic information

dopamine a form of dopa, an amino acid used in the treatment of Parkinson's disease, and found in the adrenal gland

double-blind study an experimental design used in testing the effectiveness of drugs which compares the drug in question with a placebo and, to obtain objective results, maintains both the subject's and the drug administrator's ignorance of the actual content of the substance ingested by the subject

endorphins chemicals found in the brain and recognized as the body's own painkillers, acting in a manner similar to morphine and codeine

ephedrine a bronchodilator whose actions relax smooth muscles, stimulate the heart and the central nervous system, and constrict the blood vessels

epinephrine a sympathomimetic drug used in the

134

emergency treatment of severe allergic reactions, especially to insect stings

euphoria   a mental high characterized by a sense of well-being

expectorant   a substance that facilitates or promotes the discharge of mucus from the respiratory tract accumulated during the common cold or flu

fibrocystic breast disease   an abnormal increase of fibrous connective tissue in the breast

glaucoma   an eye disease characterized by increased pressure within the eye which ultimately leads to blindness

hemorrhage   to bleed

hepatitis   inflammation of the liver, often associated with the use of contaminated hypodermic needles

hepatotoxic   causing damage to the liver

histamine   a chemical found in all body tissues that serves both as a neurotransmitter in the brain and as an important agent in inflammation and allergic reactions

hyperlipemia   an excess of fat or lipids in the blood

hypertension   high blood pressure

ibuprofen   an analgesic, anti-inflammatory, and anti-pyretic drug

International Unit   a quantity of a biological substance, such as a vitamin, that produces a particular biological effect agreed upon internationally

ischemic attacks   localized tissue anemia due to decreased blood supply

look-alikes   OTC drugs that are manufactured to look like the more potent prescription drugs

macrophage   specialized cells, present at the site of inflammation, which get rid of unwanted foreign substances and dead tissue

methapyrilene   an antihistamine previously combined with scopolamine and used as a sleep aid

myocardial infarction   heart muscle degeneration due to inadequate blood flow

narcotic   originally, a group of drugs producing effects similar to morphine; often used to refer to any substance that sedates, has a depressive effect, and/or causes dependence

nephrolithiasis   a condition characterized by having gall stones *neuron* a specialized cell, composed of a cell body, axons, and dendrites, which carries electrical messages and is the structural unit of the nervous system

neurosis a psychological disorder which originates as a mental condition, though it may come to include physiological symptoms

neurotransmitter a chemical, such as ACh, that travels from the axon of one neuron, across the synaptic gap, and to the receptor site on the dendrite of an adjacent neuron, thus allowing communication between neural cells

nitrosamines compounds that can produce cancer in the stomach

nucleotides substances important in the formation of DNA and RNA

orthomolecular psychiatry a type of therapy for mental illness that includes diets centered around mega-doses of multiple vitamins and minerals

paranoid schizophrenia a mental disorder characterized by persistent delusions, often with hallucinations

peripheral vascular occlusion the closing of superficial blood vessels, usually those supplying the legs

pernicious anemia a disorder that prevents the absorption of vitamin B_{12} into the blood stream

phenacetin an analgesic related to acetaminophen

phenylisopropylamine a class of drugs which contains amphetamine, ephedrine, and PPA

phenylpropanolamine (PPA) a sympathomimetic drug with anorectic action

phospholipid a class of large organic molecules found in all living cells in association with fats; includes lecithin

physical dependence an adaptation of the body to the presence of a drug, such that its absence produces withdrawal symptoms

placebo effect a pharmacologic effect on a symptom produced by a substance either pharmacologically inert or active only in the treatment of unrelated symptoms

premenstrual syndrome a syndrome which occurs prior to a woman's menstrual period and is characterized by fluid retention, sensitive or painful breasts, and irritability

prophylactic something that prevents or helps to prevent disease

prostaglandins chemicals released within the body during inflammation

prostate gland a gland that surrounds the male urethra into which it secretes a lubricating fluid

psychological dependence a condition in which the drug user craves a drug to maintain a sense of well-being and feels discomfort when deprived of it

psychotic behavior abnormal or pathological behavior which includes the loss of touch with reality and occasionally hallucinations and delusions

Quaaludes the trade name for methaqualone, a nonbarbiturate sedative/hypnotic

rebound congestion a condition that occurs when, after discontinuing use of a decongestant, the congestion becomes worse than it was initially

receptor sites specialized areas located on dendrites which, when bound by a sufficient number of neurotransmitter molecules, produce an electrical charge

rheumatoid arthritis a disease characterized by inflammation and swelling of the joints and often leading to stiffening and permanent disability

RNA a substance found in the cell and associated with the control of cellular chemical activities

salicylates a family of pain relievers containing salicylic acid derived from plants

scopolamine an anticholinergic with sedative, analgesic qualities, previously included in antihistamines

scurvy a disease caused by a lack of vitamin C and characterized by weakness, spongy gums, anemia, and bleeding gums and other mucous membranes

speed amphetamine

stroke a condition caused by the bursting of a blood vessel in the brain and the resultant death of that part of the brain deprived of its blood supply

sympathetic nervous system a system of nerves which, during an emergency, elicits responses of alertness, excitement, and alarm and controls the expenditure of necessary energy

sympathomimetic drug   a drug that produces effects which mimic those produced by the sympathetic nervous system

synaptic gap   the space between the axon and dendrite of two adjacent neurons in which neurotransmitters travel

synergism   when two drugs together produce effects greater than either one alone

thrombophlebitis: inflammation of a vein associated with, or due to, a thrombus, or blood clot

tolerance   a decrease of susceptibility to the effects of a drug due to its continued administration, resulting in the user's need to increase the drug dosage in order to achieve the effects experienced previously

topical drug   a drug designed for local application, such as in the form of inhalants, sprays, or drops

uppers   amphetamines

vasodilation   dilation of a blood vessel

venous thrombosis: clotting of the blood in a vein

withdrawal   the physiological and psychological effects of discontinued usage of a drug

xanthines   a class of drugs derived from the compound xanthine which naturally occurs in plants and is a central nervous system stimulant

Index

Paul Sanberg, Ph.D., an assistant professor of psychology and biomedical sciences at Ohio University, received his degree from the Australian National University in Canberra. He was a visiting scholar in the neuroscience department at the University of California and a postdoctoral fellow in the departments of neuroscience and psychiatry at The Johns Hopkins Medical School.

Richard M. T. Krema received his B.A. in pychology from Laurentian University, Ontario, and is currently a graduate student in behavioral neuroscience at Ohio University.

Solomon H. Snyder, M.D., is Distinguished Service Professor of Neuroscience, Pharmacology and Psychiatry at The Johns Hopkins University School of Medicine. He has served as president of the Society for Neuroscience and in 1978 received the Albert Laster Award in Medical Research. He has authored *Uses of Marijuana, Madness and the Brain, The Troubled Mind, Biological Aspects of Mental Disorder,* and edited *Perspective in Neuropharmacology: A Tribute to Julius Axelrod.* Professor Snyder was a research associate with Dr. Axelrod at the National Institute of Health.

Barry L. Jacobs, Ph.D., is currently a professor in the program of neuroscience at Princeton University. Professor Jacobs is author of *Serotonin Neurotransmission and Behavior* and *Hallucinogens: Neurochemical, Behavioral and Clinical Perspectives.* He has written many journal articles in the field of neuroscience and contributed numerous chapters to books on behavior and brain science. He has been a member of several panels of the National Institute of Mental Health.

Jerome H. Jaffe, M.D., formerly professor of psychiatry at the College of Physicians and Surgeons, Columbia University, has been named recently Director of the Addiction Research Center of the National Institute on Drug Abuse. Dr. Jaffe is also a psychopharmacologist and has conducted research on a wide range of addictive drugs and developed treatment programs for addicts. He has acted as Special Consultant to the President on Narcotics and Dangerous Drugs and was the first director of the White House Special Action Office for Drug Abuse Prevention.